The Middle Man

Darred Williams

ISBN 978-1-64349-263-6 (paperback)
ISBN 978-1-64349-264-3 (digital)

Christian Faith Publishing, Inc.
832 Park Avenue
Meadville, PA 16335
www.christianfaithpublishing.com

Printed in the United States of America

There are people who enter our lives and are destined to transform it. From the first time I met Dr. Williams, I was impressed with his intense desire to serve others. Over several years, Darred and I embarked on countless adventures; traveling the nation to speak of the Good News of Jesus Christ in conventions, conferences, and college and high school auditoriums. His message is both humorous and captivating, drawing on the substance of character that dwells within humanity. Darred weaves a message through divine self-actualization. He presses the audience to the jagged cliff of a complete supernatural makeover, while smiling with a "You've got this!" mindset founded by the investment of the Holy Spirit in the life of every believer.

Darred's heart for those who had difficulty in life is inspired by experience but honed through spiritual enrichment. A man who was rejected by biological parents refused to live without a full understanding of our Heavenly Father's love. A man whose very name was an example of a failure to follow through has refused to live a life of mediocrity. A man who endured intense abuse and neglect has refused to rehearse those same crimes upon those he loves and leads. How did Darred Williams accomplish this? Pursuit.

By removing all excuses and overcoming your obstacles; both seen and unseen, you, too, can rise to meet your Maker on the path of victory. That path leads to a mountain of opportunity. What is hindering your ascent? If you lack the proper tools for the climb, this author has assists for you in this book. If you lack the navigation skills to find your way, this author will guide you with the revelation of God's word to your situation. If you lack vision to see your next victory attained, allow this author to coach you into a supernatural

20/20 vision. I believe the answers you're looking for are not only in the teaching of principles, but also in the sharing of a man's story, Dr. Darred's story. Allow my friend to speak life into yours today.

Contents

Call to Adventure

At the age of twenty-nine, I've lost track of how many times I've felt insignificant, how many times I have felt like my life was worthless, how many times I have felt that nobody cared about me. Now, I know that to feel this way is foolish, that I have plenty of friends and family who care about me, love me, and whose life I have a significant role in—but sometimes, that just doesn't help.

My name is Darred Williams, and I am a twenty-nine-year-old evangelist and youth pastor. I am a single man who lives in Florida and gets an opportunity to speak to youth groups all over the state of Florida! Yes, I know that does not sound like the glamorous lifestyle you might read about in other books, especially when you pick up a book by a pastor or preacher, but that's kind of the point. At twenty-nine, everybody wants to talk to you about the "why" of life. Every sixty-year-old man wants to tell me why they are the man they are today, while every sixteen-year-old wants to ask me why I am the way I am today.

In this stage of my life, I'm less concerned about the "why" and more concerned with the "how" I want to know *how* that sixty-year-old man came to be successful in his profession; *how* he came to have his loving family; *how* he came to prepare for owning a home, getting that nice car, and preparing for retirement. I want the sixteen-year-old to understand *how* I came to the choice of job I have now, *how*

I ended up with the job I have now, *how* I plan on becoming more successful in my chosen profession, *how* I pay my bills, *how* I got my car and try to save money.

I read a lot of stories about these incredible men who did incredible things—and they talk about how they got there—but it all seems so intimidating. I have read books about men who run international corporations, pastors who lead churches of thousands, and evangelists who have traveled all over the world. How could I ever measure up to these men? How could I ever attain their level of greatness? These are immediately the first thoughts that come to mind when I read these books, and I wish that I could talk to these men when they were my age. Then, I might be able to understand how they really got there. Which is why I'm writing this book—because I am not world famous, I am not traveling the world or running a worldwide business, but I would like to one day.

So this book is to address the in-between phase of life—that awkward uncertainty that occurs between being a child that is cared for by their parents to being the adult and parent that cares for their children. Between being a kid who is only trying to be popular in school to being an adult who's trying to teach their kid that popularity isn't everything. Between being the teenage boy who struggles with idea of having sex with his girlfriend and being the man that speaks into lives of young men to help them overcome sexual sin. How do I go from one to the other? I feel like I'm caught in the middle. I'm the Middle Man.

This book contains a variety of stories of how I've gotten to where I am today, where I plan to go in my future, and how I plan to get there. During my twenty-nine years of living, I have learned a lot, and I have tried to condense all I have learned into twelve simple lessons. When I read a lot of books that try to teach something, the author spends a few paragraphs giving a personal story as an illustration, and then they spend the next twenty pages explaining to you the importance of the story and everything they want you to learn from it. This book isn't like that. It's actually the opposite; every chapter I will present the lesson learned at the very beginning and the rest of the chapter will tell various stories and experiences I've had in my life that helped me learn the lesson. Then I will end with just a few more insights about the lesson I learned.

To be completely honest, the idea of writing this book terrifies me. It's not a very flattering view, but it is an honest, and hopefully, objective look at me. This book is not like any other story where you can clearly tell you are supposed to root for the main character. There are no good guys or bad guys in these stories. There is only me, and I play both roles of good and bad. In some instances, you may feel a sense of triumph or excitement at the way I handled some experiences; while at other times, you may feel disappointed, angry or even disgusted by some of the things I have done throughout my life. So while the idea of writing this book still scares me, my hope is that the help it offers is worth the risk of being completely rejected and judged by those who read it. It's a transparent account of the sometimes greatest supporter (besides Jesus), and even more so, the greatest enemy in my life—*me.*

To some people, this book will be a waste of time. To others, it will just be an entertaining book full of some happy, sad, funny, or downright, awkward stories. My hope is that to a few people, this book would be an encouragement, a positive reinforcement that even though we all make mistakes (and believe me, you are about to read about a lot of mine), God still loves us, and He can still use us, even when we feel like we aren't good enough.

A small disclaimer before you read, I have read many books written by leaders in ministry, and they would use terminology like moral failures or falling to temptation, or even making a bad decision/mistake. While I understand why these men wrote their books that way, I believe in this day and age, we live in a world that constantly floods our youth with talks of sex, drugs, and alcohol. And they don't try to sugarcoat it in the world, so I believe they are able to handle it in the church setting as well. *So that being said . . . WARNING! If you find any of the following terms offensive, this may not be a book you will want to read*—sexual intercourse, alcohol, marijuana, oral sex, pornography, homosexuality, drug abuse, child abuse, and addictions. You have been warned. I do not want to include these terms or subjects in an attempt to add a shock factor, but simply to be as real and honest as possible so there will be no confusion or uncertainty as to what I'm talking about.

All other business aside, thank you for taking time to look through this book, and I hope the stories in it serve you well!

1

What Doesn't Kill You . . . Still Hurts

Most people who want to reminisce about their childhood go to the closet and pull out the old photo album. They brush off the dust from the front cover and open it to find pictures of smiling faces—pictures of family, parents, and grandparents along with them as small children and babies. For me, there really is no need to reminisce, and there are no photo albums. Just one very large envelope filled not with pictures, but paperwork. Rather than having a bunch of pictures of my mother when she was young, all I have of her is a photocopy of her driver's license; and instead of pictures of my father, all I have to remember him by is a copy of a letter he left explaining why he abandoned me and my brother. You see, I was adopted. My mother had me when she was sixteen years old, and my father wasn't much of a father. H was more like the man that gave me my Y chromosome. My mother had a severe drug problem—basically, she loved taking drugs more than she liked taking care of children. And my father had a law problem—basically, he didn't like to follow it. So those are my parents, a drug-addict and a criminal. Not exactly an ideal atmosphere to raise a child. Unfortunately, this didn't matter to my biological mother and father, as they ended up having another son eighteen months after I was born—my brother, Darian.

My parents attempted to take care of my brother and I, but like I said before, it wasn't their top priority. After less than two years after my birth, my father decided that the responsibility of two sons was too much to bear. My father left us in the company of some "friends" of his, which might have turned out to be the best decision he could have made as a person but might possibly have been the worst decision he ever made as a father. He left us in the company of three people, with nothing more than the following letter:

To Whom this letter may concern:

I, the father, of one Darren King Hayes Jr. and also Darian Michael Hayes. I hereby am leaving them in the custody of one, Shawn _____, two Chester _____, and third Angela Marie _____ until I can care for them. The reason for this is because their mother is neglecting them. She [is] out of the house because of her refusal to come home in the evenings. Of the days she's sleeping often. If she tries to reclaim them she cannot. The so-called mother Nicole admitted to having problems with drugs. Her actual name is Arlene Lee _____. Records indicate as always running away from problems. If she come[s] back while I, the father, am at work she is not to take them. The authorities should be called to investigate her whereabouts if she returns.

Darren King

I know my father was doing what he thought was right, and in the long run, it was definitely the best decision for both me and my brother. I mean, like I said earlier, they were not ready to be parents. For example, on my nose, I have a scar that runs all the way down my left nostril. For the longest time, I had no idea how I got this scar. Until I discovered (how I discovered this, I still can't remember) that one day my mom went shopping when I was a baby and left me on top of the car in my car seat as she drove off. I fell off and was luckily enough to have this scar as the only reminder of that accident. So I understand why my father decided to leave us, but it still hurts to think that the man who gave me life didn't want to be a part of my life. I am stronger now because of what my father did, but his choice to give us up would lead to hardships in my life no child should have to deal with, ever.

Of course, as I am sure you can tell, unlike my father's letter stated, he did not come back for my brother and I; and within a few days, we were placed into foster care with HRS (Health and Rehabilitative Services). For the next few years, my life was a blur of foster parents, group homes, and visitations with my mother. I don't remember anything about my mom. The only memory I actually have of her is one time when we were visiting her, and she had a SEGA Genesis and my brother and I played Sonic. I don't actually remember her or what she looked like. All I can remember is that my young brain couldn't comprehend how to get Sonic to go all the way around the full circle, so I would let my mother do it for me. This lack of my relationship with my biological mother definitely had a negative impact on my ability relate to the opposite gender, but we'll get to that later.

Many people would think that getting out of that horrible situation at a young age would make life so much better for my brother and I, but before things got better, they got worse—a lot worse. I don't remember all the foster families/group homes I was in; I was really young of course. The first foster family I remember being a part of was a nice-looking suburban family. They had children of their own, so I had other kids to play with. I don't remember much of life in that home; the only thing I do remember vividly were the beatings. It wasn't so much the brutality of being beat, but the consistency of them. I remember being so afraid to do anything wrong because I knew that no matter how insignificant the offense, I knew that a whooping was coming. Things like not saying "Thank you" or "You're welcome" or having you clothes inside out in the laundry would cause the father to come at you with his belt. It wasn't all bad ₒh. I did have a birthday with that family, and I remember getting my first video game on that birthday. It was a handheld racing game that wasn't that great, but it was the first present I ever remember getting so I definitely appreciated it. I don't remember how long I stayed at that home, but I eventually moved on.

The next house I stayed at was definitely the worst experience I ever had during my childhood. It was the only group home experience that I can remember. It was a boys' group home, and there were about eight boys that were staying there. The house "father" was a man who owned a restaurant, and the house "mother" was a lady who pretty much lived on the couch. I use the terms *father* and *mother* very loosely because their presence was pretty much not felt at all. The "father" worked nonstop at his restaurant, while the "mother" would sit on the couch all day and send all the boys outside to "play" until the sun went down. Of the eight young men, I was among the youngest (I do believe that there was one younger than me), and I don't remember my brother being there. The older boys' idea of playing was to set up fights between the younger boys and cheering them on. (We were the original Fight Club). If you refused to fight, they would find ways to motivate you. Whether it was you getting beaten down by the older boys or refusing to give you any of the snacks that were provided and distributed by the older boys, it didn't matter, if they wanted you to fight, you fought. When the fighting wasn't enough, they would use us younger boys to gratify their sexual needs. Yes, this was my life at the age of five—nonstop physical violence and sexual abuse.

If that wasn't enough, our house was also the punching bag of the neighborhood. Other boys in the neighborhood could not stand us (I am still not sure why), so we would get into fights all the time (maybe that's why the older boys felt the need to train us every day). On one occasion, the neighborhood boys decided they did not want to fight us, so they threw rocks at us instead. We were all stuck outside, and the house seemed a million miles away. As I attempted to make a run for it, I was the unlucky one. A sharp rock hit me in the face, and blood flooded out of my cheek. I was so scared that I was going to get in trouble, I did not even go to tell the "mother." I hid in the bedroom as the blood continued to flow. The other boys eventually told her, and I spent a good six to eight hours in the emergency room. I still have the scar on my cheek to remind me of that experience, as well as a whole bunch of other ones to remind me of the house.

This experience is also my first memory of questioning who God is and if He is really real. The house parents of the group home were Muslims, and they believed the boys should be as well. They taught us how to pray the Muslim way. (We washed our hands and feet before prayer. Each kid had a prayer rug. We all had to face in a certain direction, and there were a series of poses and phrases we would do.) I was so bitter and angry at my situation that I blamed it on Allah (the Muslim word for God), and I prayed because I knew I would get beat up if I didn't join in. But let's just say I was very creative with what I would say in the prayer phrases under my breath.

I don't think I would have made through that experience if not for one decision I made when I first got to the group home. It was early on when I first got to the home, and I was being introduced to the routine and rules of the house. I was told I had to fight, and I had refused, which caused me to have to beat down by the older boys. They also took the bologna sandwich that was for me, rubbed it in the dirt, and forced me to eat it. I remember crawling on the ground on my hands and feet when the beating was over and pulling myself up on the swing set. As I sat down on the swing, tears in my eyes, I pressed my hands flat together and prayed. I don't know how I learned to do it. I don't know why I decided to do it, but I prayed a very short, but desperate prayer as if my life depended on it (because I truly believed that it did). The boys made fun of me and the way I prayed, saying it was impossible for God to hear me like that and how He didn't care about me. In the end, my prayer was just that God would take me away from this place, from this situation; that I did not belong here. I was praying for God to remove me from that home, and I believe that God took that prayer to another level and was setting me up to remove me from foster care. The first time I prayed might have been the most important prayer I ever prayed and was probably the prayer that saved my life.

Eventually, all the boys were removed from that home. Later on in life, I would find out that it was because foster care would eventually find out about all the abuse that took place in that house. I like to think that my prayer was the reason for that. The next home I was moved to was an elderly African American couple. It was the only home where I remember having my younger brother, Darian, with me. My brother and I were the only two children in this home. The parents, who to us, felt more like grandparents, did have an older son I believe, but he had moved out on his own. That was probably the best foster-care experience I can remember. I can remember my brother and I playing with all our toys, which we pulled out of the trash bag of our belongings, not a good memory, I remember going to church on Sunday mornings and going to restaurants like the local pancake house after church. I remember being in the kids' choir (the only song I can remember is "Inside Out" and to this day, I can't find anyone that knows that song).

It was a pleasant life for my brother and I, especially after everything we had been through, but I still felt empty and incomplete. This wasn't the life I wanted. It was almost too peaceful, and I was a product of chaos—not meaning that I wanted to cause chaos, but I just needed more excitement.

That excitement came in the form of two strangers that we would have dinner with one night. Their names were Michael and Dawn Williams, and they were from West Palm Beach. One night, after an evening service at church, our "foster grandparents" took us out to eat at the Pancake House (I'm pretty sure that's not the name of it, but I do remember them serving pancakes.); and our foster care case worker, Bernard, was there with these two adults—Michael and Dawn. Bernard spent some time introducing us to them, and we talked for a while. And then Bernard explained that our "grandparents" would be going on vacation, so we would be spending a week with Michael and Dawn down in West Palm Beach.

Now you have to understand, my brother and I had only ever lived in Tampa and St. Petersburg, so West Palm Beach sounded like this exotic utopia we just had to see, so we were thrilled. It wasn't too long after that we packed up our bags, said goodbye to "Grandma" and "Grandpa," and Bernard drove us the four hours south. We didn't know it at the time, but that would be the last time we would see that couple who cared for us. And we were on our way to our new home.

Now I don't tell you these stories in hopes that you would sympathize my childhood, or that you might feel sorry for me—and I didn't finish with our trip to West Palm Beach so that this chapter can have a happy ending (because, believe me, this story is far from over). I told this story so you might understand one simple truth that has taken me over twenty years to learn, which is very simply this—everybody hurts.

Everyone you have ever met, everyone you have ever encountered, everyone you walk or drive by has some sort of hurt in his or her life. Statistics says that 25 percent of children will be sexually abused by the age of ten; 50 percent of all marriages end in divorce; and 25 percent of people will struggle with alcoholism or drug addiction. That's already 100 percent, and yes, some of these categories may overlap. But these statistics don't include people who deal with the death of a loved one, people who live in poverty, families where one parent has abandoned them, children with parents in prison, children in foster care, pornography addiction, sex trafficking, gang affiliation, or sexual orientation/gender confusion. I guarantee that when it comes to people in this world, everyone has dealt with at least one of these issues or one of so many others I have not even mentioned.

We have all heard it said before that what doesn't kill you makes you stronger, but I'm here to tell you this doesn't mean it still doesn't hurt to bring it up. I have had the opportunity to share my testimony multiple times on various stages in front of thousands of people (not because of who I am, but because of the relationships God has blessed me with—but we'll get to that later). And yes, while I feel pretty strong in the idea that these hardships have made me into the man I am today, I still feel the pain of being that five-year-old kid getting beaten up when I share. I still have to fight back the tears when I start to talk about the father that abandoned me. Yes, it's easier than it has been in the past, but it still hurts.

The biggest difference is that I strive to be a person with hurts and not a person who's hurting. The difference between the two is that a person with hurts uses those pains and hardships to propel him or her forward, to move toward a greater purpose. While a person who's hurting dwells in his or her pain and lets it consume them, and they can't move on to anything else because all they know is that pain. And they don't know how to get past it.

I know there is only one way to get past that pain, and his name is Jesus. The Bible says in Isaiah 53:5, "But he was pierced for our transgressions, he was crushed for our iniquities; the punishment that brought us peace was on him, and by his wounds we are healed."

This means that Jesus went through all the pain on the cross so he can take all the pain we deal with in life. God knew that if He didn't give us a way out of our pain, it would take us over; so He gave us His son Jesus, who was so perfect that he couldn't be consumed by any hurt. All we have to do is give it to him. There's no way I could write a book, speak at a church, or do anything important without doing this next part.

The sacrifice Jesus made was a gift, and just like any other gift, we have to accept it. If somebody gave you a birthday gift, and you just left it there, it wouldn't be of any use. The same thing goes with Jesus's gift. Unless we accept his sacrifice, it's useless.

Maybe you're reading this book and thinking that you're not sure if you've accepted this gift or that you are a person who is hurting and want to give it to Jesus. The great thing is that you can do it right now. All you have to do is say the following prayer out loud and direct it up to heaven (you don't have to physically look up to heaven, but just know that you are saying these words to God):

Heavenly Father,
I know that I am a sinner,
I know that I have a lot of hurts in my life.
I also know that you sent you son, Jesus,
to die for my sins and my hurts.
I accept Jesus into my life,
And believe in my heart that after he died on the cross,
He rose from the dead three days later.
I thank you Jesus for the price you paid for me,

And I ask that you would come into my heart and life.
In Jesus's name,
Amen.

It's as simple as that. As long as you believed that God heard that prayer and that Jesus is real, well, my friend, you are on your way to the great life. At a lot of churches, the pastor will do his altar call and this prayer at the end of the service, but I decided to do it at the beginning of this book because it truly is a new beginning. This is just the first step—and I know there are some reading this book that already know these things—but this is for the ones that didn't and just accepted Jesus.

So if you already know Jesus as your Lord and Savior, would you take a moment to just celebrate with me all the lives that God has impacted just from these last few paragraphs? (This is the part of the service where the crowd participates with a cry of praise. Hallelujahs are acceptable.) And if you just said that prayer and accepted Jesus for the first time, let me be the first to congratulate you on the most important decision of your life! There are other steps that you need to take. Unfortunately, this book does not address those specifically, so I would highly suggest that you find a church in your community (immediately! Don't wait till Sunday or keep reading!) and tell them about the commitment you just made, and they will be able to help you. Once you've done that, come back and join me as we move on to chapter 2.

2

Time Heals All Wounds . . .
but Still Leaves Scars

When we arrived at the house of Michael and Dawn Williams, it was like heaven on earth for two young boys. It was two and a half acres of land with trees to climb, a pond, a two-story house with five bedrooms, and most importantly, a trampoline! My brother and I could not believe how lucky we were; this was going to be the best week ever! We loved this place, and we were going to make the most of it.

Along with the awesome yards (front and backyard!) and the awesome house, we also had other kids to play with. There were also two other sisters at the house, Kristy and Jamie, who were two and four years old, and another girl Donna, who was a teenager in high school.

I don't remember that week, it flew by so quickly; but before the week was over, I remember the phone call from our caseworker, Bernard. I grabbed the phone from Michael and answered. Bernard asked how I was doing at down in West Palm Beach, and of course, I told him it was awesome. Then he told me how he was planning on get me and my brother plane tickets this time around so we wouldn't have to drive! I was so excited! I had never been on a plane before, and after this incredible week, my first time on a plane would definitely be the icing on the cake.

Then Bernard threw in the monkey wrench. As soon as he finished he sentence about the plane, he continued on by saying, "Unless you want to stay there?" I hadn't thought of that for a second. I could stay here? For how long? Why? Did the Williams family know about this? All these questions began to race through my head, but as quickly as they raced in, they disappeared. What did that matter? I was a kid and I loved this place, so in my infinite, seven-year-old cleverness, I responded back to him, "Bernard, you can hold on to my plane ticket because I'm staying here." That decision would almost completely shape the direction of the rest of my life—for the better, of course.

Eventually, I would come to find out that our trip to West Palm Beach was never meant to be a temporary fix; this was to be a permanent solution. Michael and Dawn Williams wanted to adopt us. They wanted us to be a part of their family. Long story short, we ended up getting adopted (yeah, I realize I really jumped the gun on a very important part of my life, but I was a kid and things like this just kind of fly by. It was still a really big deal to me, I promise.), and throughout this process, I would come to learn that Kristy and Jamie were also in the process of being adopted, while Donna was Dawn's daughter. Also, during that time, they added another teenage boy to the family, Greg.

Now I don't remember the first time I started calling Michael and Dawn Mom and Dad, but I do remember the first time I realized they were my parents.

We were all doing some sort of family activity, and I had done something wrong. Michael then disciplined me by spanking me. (I don't remember the type of hit. I just remember getting hit.) And I was definitely more startled than hurt. I then proclaimed to him he couldn't hit me. I knew the law—foster parents couldn't abuse their kids. And I will never forget my father's response. He said, "That's where you're wrong, buddy. You're mine now."

It's a very weird nostalgic memory to have, my first time being beaten, but it was the first time anyone had ever told me that I was theirs. That was a huge deal.

Yes, I remember all the questions I had to answer, all the paperwork that had to be filled out, standing in the courtroom, and going through the proceedings of getting adopted; but for me, Michael and Dawn Williams became my parents the moment they were willing to take ownership of me. It was then that I felt most comfortable and most protected. For the first time in my life, I felt like I was a part of a family.

Unfortunately, while we had an understanding of what it was to be a part of this created family, a lot of other people didn't understand it at all; specifically, some of my peers and classmates.

When I moved down to West Palm Beach, I started at a new school, which meant trying to make new friends. I first started at my new school, Egret Lake Elementary, in the third grade; and in the beginning, it was great. I made a few friends, even had my first birthday party (yeah, I was turning nine and just having my first birthday party)—we went to a skating rink. Fourth grade was about the same. I had my first crush during that time (her name was Heather), and I had the first person to have a crush on me (oddly enough, also named Heather, but a different one).

I never told Heather (the one I liked) that I liked her, but Heather (the one who liked me) didn't have the same reservations. I remember going to my desk and looking inside to find a notebook paper covered in hearts and butterflies, with bold letters proclaiming, "Darred, I love you, baby!" I flipped the paper over to find out it was from Heather! You can imagine my disappointment when I discovered that it wasn't from the Heather that I hoped it was from. Anyways, fourth grade went easily, but once fifth grade came around, things began to get difficult.

Now, you have to understand that to me, adoption was a pretty common thing. I didn't think it was anything to be ashamed of or sad about. On the contrary, I was proud to be part of a family that loved me so much they chose me! So I had no reservations with telling people I was adopted—why should I? They don't have any problems telling me their parents gave birth to them. (Just for the record, nobody has ever bragged to me that their parents gave birth to them. Just trying to make a point.)

So basically, it was no secret that my younger brother and I were adopted at Egret Lake. So by the time fifth grade rolls around, things are going smoothly. I became a safety patrol. I was in the gifted program. (Basically, it was the smart kids who needed more interactive activities and assignments to challenge them more.) I finally overcame my lisp, thanks to a speech therapist working with me for the past two years. (I had a severe lisp when I was younger because of the fluid in my ears, so I had to have surgery to get tubes in my ears to drain the fluid when I was a baby. But it affected the way I said the letter *s*. Lots of saliva all the time, not pretty, but also not important. Moving on . . .)

Everything was going well for me, and the good times kept coming. In the spring of my fifth-grade year, the safety patrols were having their annual trip to Washington, DC, and I couldn't be more excited! To this day, I can't tell you where my interest in politics originated from; all I know is that I loved it. (Actually, I got a degree in political science when I went to college, but the problem is that even though I love politics, I hated the politicians.) So this trip to me was a dream come true. Little did I know it would turn into my worst nightmare come to life.

So we were on our way to Washington via train, and I loved every minute of it. Not only were we going to the head of political activity in our country, but it was my first overnight trip! We got to pick our roommates, so I choose two of my friends, Derek and Atif. Now, one thing you have to understand about me, especially as a kid, is that I'm very active, and loud, and some people might even use a word like *obnoxious*. Now as I have grown and matured, this obnoxious, loud behavior has mellowed out over time. (some people might say not enough, but the Bible says, "Judge not lest ye be judged.")

We made it through one day before Derek and Atif were completely done with me. Yes, between the train ride, getting to the hotel, and having dinner, my two roommates had all the Darred they could handle. As you can imagine, this can place quite a strain on our relationship during this five-day trip.

While I was having the time of my life, my personality began to wear out some, if not all, of my peers. For them, this was just a time to walk around somewhere new and get away from their family for a few days. But for me, it was so much more.

By the end of the trip, all the boys had decided they had enough of me. (During a lot of the activities, boys and girls were separated, so the girls didn't have to deal with me as much.) So on the train-ride home, in my excited state, I had finally pushed one of the boys over the edge. While proudly talking about how amazing the trip was, the boy jumped up and screamed, "Enough! Now I know why your parents didn't want you!"

These few words cut deeper than any blade ever could, but not nearly as much the laughter of each and every boy in our train car. (Boys and girls were in separate cars.) My entire psyche was shattered. This entire time I carried my adoption like a proud badge of honor, when in fact, everyone looked at it as something to be ashamed of. I had thought for so long that I was chosen, but in fact, everyone around me viewed me as a mistake that had been discarded.

I leapt out of my seat and tried to attack that boy who had shown me how worthless I was, but the other boys holding me back quickly overwhelmed me. In my blinded rage, I flung myself to the back of the train car with the luggage and threw my body on top of them, my cheeks burning as they were covered with hot tears of anger.

I don't know how long I lay there or when the teachers came back into the car to discover the emotional wreck that was lying on the luggage. They couldn't get any sort of explanation as to what happened from me or any of the other boys.

Toward the end of the trip, the teachers give pins to each of the students as a small reward of their service as a safety patrol. The only thing they had to do was get the approval of all the other students. So the teacher would get each student and tell them each name of their classmates, and all the students had to do was say yes or no to that person getting the pin. Now, this was more of a formality than anything else. The teachers never really expected anyone not to receive the pin. You only needed half of your classmates to say yes. Yet you can probably guess the only patrol that didn't get the required number of votes. That's right, yours truly.

When my name was called to go get my pin, the teachers pulled me aside and explained to me that too many of my classmates didn't think I deserved this pin, but that my peers didn't understand everything that I had went through, so they were going to give it to me anyway. After the earlier incident, this blow took me out. As I walked back to my seat, carrying that pin that I knew in my heart I didn't deserve; part of me died in that moment.

A sad, depressed boy who thought he was worth nothing replaced the joyful, exuberant young man who was so excited at finally having a new life and family. Not even an insignificant piece of plastic in the form of a medal could change how terrible I felt. Even though I had a family, I once again felt worthless.

You see, even though I had a different life and a different mindset, there were still old wounds that affected me. When I was in foster care, everything around me was a constant reminder about how nobody wanted me. When I was finally adopted, I thought that those days and thoughts were finally over; and even though I had moved on from that situation in the natural, I still had to deal with it emotionally and mentally. The same thing happens when we become a Christian. A lot of people believe that once you make that prayer to commit your life to Christ your entire life changes. And while that is true, the part of your life that changes is you and how you approach situations, not necessarily the situation.

Many people expect that giving their life to Jesus makes all their problems go away, but the Bible doesn't say that when we are "born again" (which is a fancy term for allowing Jesus to take control of our life), that our lives would get better. It says that when we are born again, we are a new creation, meaning that we don't react the same way to the same situation as we did in the past. As a new creation, God gives us new ways to react.

If I understood this idea when I was in the fifth grade, I wouldn't have been so angry with my classmate. I would have understood that though the world might look at me one way, the one who loves me and created me (God!) blessed me with these incredible parents and this incredible new life, and that it didn't matter where I came from because He was putting me somewhere great. The world will try to bring up your past to make you feel like you're worthless. The devil will lie to you and try to say that you aren't worth anything because of what you may have done before you knew God, before you were adopted into His family, but it is important to know that the world and the devil can't define you—only God can define you.

We will go more into this idea in a later chapter. For now, it is most important that you understand that you can't allow your past wounds to deter you from where you're going. I'm not telling you they're not going to hurt, or that you won't have to deal with past hurts, but that these hurts and wounds do not need to prevent you from the great things that God has for you.

The Bible says in Jeremiah 29:11, "For I know the plans I have for you' declares the Lord, 'plans to prosper you and not to harm you, plans to give you hope and a future." So you see, it doesn't matter what you went through or what you've done, God always has great plans for you.

So no matter what people might throw in your face, no matter what scar or wound may be opened again, you can find joy in the fact that God has a plan for you that is greater than any of those scars because, as I talked about at the end of the last chapter, he took on all that pain so that we wouldn't have to. I would encourage you at this time to think about anything from your past that might still have an old wound or scar that when brought up makes you feel hurt or worthless. If there is anything, take some time to give it up to God, telling Him that His plans and desires and love for you are greater than any hurt that you have gone through and truly believing that.

3

⟡

Bad Things Happen . . . (Period)

I've learned a very valuable lesson in my twenty-nine years on this earth, and it has helped me cope with difficult times of my life. At some point, everybody feels like the Middle Man. It doesn't matter how successful you are, how much money you have, or how popular you are—eventually, you're going to feel like you're caught in the middle.

Being the Middle Man is not just the idea of being in the middle; it's the feeling of being overlooked or neglected that adds to it. Being the Middle Man is that overwhelming desire for attention because it seems like everyone around you thinks you're insignificant. Just like a middle child looks for the adoration that the baby of the family gets and the praise that the oldest sibling gets, so do people in different stages of life feel left out in the cold.

There is no specific time for someone to get this Middle Man syndrome; anyone at any point in their life can feel like the middle by simply comparing themselves to others around them. A college student can feel in the middle by being overlooked by the high school up-and-comers around him and the young professionals with college degrees and careers. A young professional can feel neglected when the attention goes to a new recruit, coming in for a job with a promising education and all the praise goes to the managers above him. A parent/child can feel neglected when their children love the grandparents more and their parents are concerned only with spending time with their grandchildren. I've learned that it's not a question of "if" you're going to feel caught in the middle, but a matter of "when."

The first time that I found myself in the role of the Middle Man was during the three most horrendous years of my life. I spent time in a hellish gulag filled with psychological torture, incessant ridicule, emotional turmoil, and mental anguish. I spent three years in this prison with no hope of escape, a place filled with bloodthirsty companions and cutthroat competitors and ruthless persecutors. My only silver lining the idea that my sentence would eventually end, and I would be able to move on.

Many people call this place middle school. For me, it was hell.

Now if you recall, my elementary school career ended horribly. I was ridiculed, ostracized, and cast out because of my status as an adopted child. So when middle school rolled around, I took the exact opposite approach I had taken in elementary school.

Rather than be proud and bold and tell everyone about how I was adopted and chosen into my family, I wouldn't tell anyone about being adopted. As a matter of fact, I decided not to tell anyone anything. There was no reason for me to give any of these new students any information into my life. I had already seen firsthand that children were cruel and any inside information that these kids had on me would just be ammunition they would eventually use to destroy me.

Turns out, these kids didn't need any of my life story; they had plenty of ammo just by looking at me.

I should explain something before I continue. When I was a child, my dad had one major pet peeve about young people that he made sure would never occur with his children. And that peeve was sagging pants and showing underwear. To him, this was a carnal sin that deserved capital punishment.

So my dad had a brilliant way to combat this epidemic so it would never invade his home. Pants that fit firmly on us so they would always remain on the waist (pretty much, pants that were too tight), along with shirts that extended lower than necessary to prevent any view of unnecessary "backside cracks." (Basically, if the shirts were too big, and somehow, we managed to overcome the first barrier and get our pants below our waist. The baggy shirt would cover up any undergarment showings.) Add this with the desire and suggestion of my father that we always have our shirts tucked in, you having the makings of a twelve-year-old boy with too-tight pants and too-baggy shirt that made me look like a pterodactyl with flamingo legs!

Yeah, I was begging to get picked on. My first impression in middle school didn't help either. On my first day, I woke up excited and ready for a fresh start. So I put on my uniform (with a shirt two sizes too big and pants three sizes too small), grabbed my book bag with wheels and handle so I could roll it (yeah, I was that guy!) and got dropped off at the bus stop. Only to discover . . . that our school did not require uniforms!

Yes, the first impression I made in middle school was a school-uniform-wearing pterodactyl with curly, extremely messy, curly hair and a severe acne problem. You can see now why my middle school classmates had everything they needed to destroy me.

If that wasn't enough, my mannerisms and interests just added more fuel to the fire. As a twelve-year-old boy, my interest in girls hadn't fully developed, so my other interests overpowered it. These interests were any Japanese cartoon that dealt with monsters being trained by kids (Pokémon, Digimon, etc.), role-playing video games, comic book heroes, and reading books. While these interests are not at all bad or negative, I quickly learned that you weren't supposed to make it known that these were the things you were interested in, or it was open season for you to be ridiculed.

Rather than spend my time at lunch conversing with friends or joking with classmates, I sat at the end of the lunch table with my Digimon trading cards or slaving over video game strategy guides or reading the latest Hardy Boys book I had picked up from the library. This opened the door for any young man that wanted to make him feel better about himself by putting me down, and believe me, there were plenty of them.

The main culprits were John and Jonah. Between the two of them, I saw one of them in just about every class I had, plus John and I rode the same bus home. So they attacked me with a relentless assault of verbal attacks, attempts to provoke me into violence, and endless streams of insults. I took it all in stoic silence. I didn't have the personal confidence or clever speech to come back at them, so I hoped that if I didn't react they would eventually become bored with me and move on.

The problem was I felt as if there was no one I could turn to that could help me with my issue. I did not have any real friends at school, so there was no one there that could relate or support me. I was the child who got the good grades and didn't get into trouble, so it seemed like my parents were too busy being concerned with my older brother, Greg, who was having some behavioral issues, or my younger siblings Kristy and Darian who just didn't do as well in school as me. So they were no help.

The only people I felt somewhat close to were the kids I went to church with that were children of my parents' Bible study members. Yet our relationship was superficial and all about having fun together. I didn't want to ruin that by bringing in all this emotional drama to our carefree lifestyle. So for five days a week, eight hours a day, I was imprisoned in a jail cell of loneliness where the guards were twelve-, thirteen-, and fourteen-year-old boys who continually asserted their dominance over me. This would be my life for three long, impossibly difficult years.

Now at this point, I'm sure you're thinking there's no way things can get any worse, but I can assure you that if you're thinking that, you are 100 percent wrong. If middle school was not already awkward and terrible enough, let's throw in puberty, just for fun. Puberty had hit me somewhere around the sixth grade, so it came with of the normal signs of the times: cracking voice, body hair growing in places other than my head, weird "physiological" things happening to me—you know, the usual.

The school decided they should take on the responsibility of teaching us what these changes meant. My dad had other ideas. So when the topic of sexual education came up, it did nothing to improve my reputation or stature.

I remember bringing home the permission slip to get signed in order to actually sit in the class. (I don't know if they still do this, but back then, they needed permission from parents to teach about sex.)

I brought it to my dad, and he read over it, went, and got a blank piece of paper and proceeded to write an essay in response. What the essay said, I will never know, not because I did not look, but simply because I could not read his handwriting. My science teacher did not seem to share the same inability to interpret my father's penmanship.

The class was told beforehand that if our parents did not want us in the class, other arrangements would be made for us. I found out that those arrangements consisted of me (being the only student whose parent refused to allow him to be a part of the class) sitting on a stool outside of the portable for two different days. And I thought life was bad before! Now it seemed like the entire school knew I was the only student who was not "sexually educated."

I had never felt so alone or abandoned in my entire life.

Even though I did not learn about sex in the classroom, I did receive somewhat of an informal education about the topic later on from classmates. I do not remember all the details, but it was sometime in the seventh grade that a couple of the boys introduced me to the idea of masturbation (though they used much more colorful terms, that I will refrain from using here). When I look back on it, their conversation was quite inane.

They were basically staring down girls in our class and bragging about how they would be using those girls' images to satisfy themselves that night. Like I said, they were idiotic. With that being said, I took that information and decided to try it out that night. I did not even understand what I was fully doing (Because once again, I was the one kid in the Roosevelt Middle School class of 2002 who did not go to the sex ed classes), but I did know that after I did that, it felt good. And quite honestly, with everything going so terribly in my life, I was ecstatic that anything in my life could actually still feel good.

Now, you may be questioning why I would even put this very uncomfortable and awkward topic in this book. And I kind of explained that in the opening, but I wanted to take a moment to elaborate. I feel like I am not the first preteen to accidentally stumble on the physical satisfaction of masturbation. I did not think I was lusting after girls, or being impure, or violating these girls and their bodies with my mind, I just thought I was making myself feel good. Eventually, it did evolve into these extreme levels of impurity and led to struggles with sex and pornography, but we will hold off on that for a later chapter.

As a young man, I have learned that you have to meet students with where they are at, and that means dealing with the simplicity of masturbation as they view it. We can rant and monologue all day long about the dangers of lust and impurity, but first, we have to recognize the way teenagers view it. And the simplest way I can express that is by explaining how I looked at it as a teenager.

The first time I masturbated, all it took was the physical action to get the physical satisfaction. Yet as time went on, I found myself having to get more mentally engaged, imagining girls and situations, and corrupting my mind. Eventually, this evolution would move on to much more detrimental actions.

Can I be honest? The young boy or girl who just discovered masturbation does not view it as the most heinous sin and grievous act of impurity that adults know that it can become. So before we go into our discussion about the dangers of it, we should spend time making sure our children understand that it evolves, and something that may start off as seemingly innocent can lead to downfall.

The alcoholic did not think their first drink would ruin their life. The drug addict did not know that his or her first joint would completely destroy them. The same way that the young teenage boy or teenage girl does not understand that one physical act can complete destroy their purity, shatter their future marriage, and corrupt their view of the opposite sex for years to come.

It would be easy to wrap up this chapter with the major lesson of it, which is (in case you've forgotten) that bad things happen (period!), but I wanted to leave this chapter with just a little glimmer of hope. Because with as bad as middle school was for me, there were some positives that came out of it, which partially goes along with the lesson, because even in the midst of your worst situations, there can be some good that comes from it. So before I go over the purpose of these stories, I wanted to talk about the two brightest moments of my middle school career.

The first one had to have been my English class. If you recall, I was a somewhat intelligent student, but English was by far my favorite subject during my middle school career. This was because of the escape that it gave me, and that escape came in the form of my English journal.

For my seventh and eighth grade year, my English teacher was Ms. Wilson, and she allowed each student to have a journal for the class and give us various writing assignments to include in the journal. Some of them were commenting on historical quotes, providing summaries on passages read in class, but my favorite was definitely the opportunities that we had to create stories on our own. In the midst of the cruel and unusual punishment of adolescent, the only reprieve I truly found was when I completely changed my life and situation in the work of a narrative.

This was part of the reason why middle school was the cultivation of my addiction to video games. In the real world, nobody cared about me. Nobody looked to me for help. No one thought I mattered, but in the video game, I was the hero. I became really involved in RPGs (role-playing games) during this time, and one of the best features I found was I could change the names of the characters as I saw fit.

So the main protagonist (hero, for those who don't know. Please pay attention to your English teachers!) was obviously myself. While the hero's love interest became whatever young lady took my fancy during that part of the school year. (It was basically a revolving door of girls' names: Heather, Ruthy, Sheri, Samantha, Heather again—you get the idea.) And as sad as this may sound, the other characters always kept their names because I did not have any friends close enough that they could join me on my most recent quest to save the newest, imaginary, digitalized world that Final Fantasy had just created. Yet I digress . . . Back to Ms. Wilson's class.

It was during my stint in middle school English that I figured out one of my greatest talent—the ability to write well. (Yeah, I see the irony of an author writing about how good he is at writing, but hey, you're still reading the book, so what does that say?)

I would turn in my journal each week, only to receive the highest praise from Ms. Wilson soon after. She adored my stories and was more than willing to share that adoration with me. At first, I thought that was simply her way of being an encouragement to all her students, but as more time went on, I began to see that her praise was primarily exclusive to me. And it made me feel great.

For everything I had accomplished in elementary school and everything I endured in the mandated juvenile detention center that everyone is forced to attend from ages twelve to fourteen (or for some, fifteen. I'm not judging. Just saying.), it felt great to be good at something. So I poured over this journal, invested my heart and soul into the tales I weaved on those pages, partially in hope that someday these fantasies of praise and attention of me might actually one day become a reality.

This hope is probably what led to my second major moment of my life during this time. With school so bad and utterly hopeless, my social life consisted of one major source: the church. My parents were firm believers that the church is where the family should be, so Jamie, Kristy, Darian, Greg, and I found ourselves at the church twice a week (Sundays and Wednesdays), along with weekly meetings with our cell (Life? Deeper? Cadre? I've been around church so long these groups all have different names. But all seek to serve the same purpose—to bring members of the church closer together.) groups once a week.

So I dived into the church atmosphere because it was truly a sanctuary. When everyone was mean to me Monday through Friday from 7:30 AM to 4:00 PM, I found that everyone I encountered at Trinity Church International was generally nice on Sunday mornings and Wednesday evenings. And my parents were so involved that interacting with these people was pretty consistent.

My parents would even host a Labor Day party every year for the vast majority of the church. It was during one of these parties during my seventh-grade party that I received attention from a girl (Ruthy, who would later become a recurring character in my video game adventures) for the first time since Heather from fourth grade. It was also during that party I received my first kiss (Angela) from a game of Truth or Dare with a few of the kids—embarrassing I know, but it's the truth. This led to my first experience in middle-school drama (long story short: I liked Ruthy; my cousin Dudley, participator of the aforementioned game of Truth or Dare, thought I liked Angela and tried to play matchmaker. In the end, Darred ends up alone with the only relationship being lived out on his PlayStation).

Wow, I got way off track there, but that's life. Anyhow, there was one specific night I was going to the youth group (which was a huge deal to seventh grade me, as I'm sure it is for most seventh graders. If you're in seventh grade, and it's not a big deal to you, give me a break. I was not as cool as I am sure you are.) and we had a special speaker named Mark Murray. My parents knew Mark, and I knew he was some sort of coach at the school. Coach Mark (that's what we called him) preached some message—I cannot recall what he talked about—but I will never forget the end of the night. Coach Mark asked that if anyone had a gift with words, he wanted to pray with them. I knew right away this was for me (but I also knew the mentality of teenagers, if ever they are told that they have a gift, everyone thinks it for them) so before I could hesitate, I stood up and almost ran up to the altar. I had never done this before. In a room of a hundred teenagers who are almost all older than you, the last thing you want to do is draw attention to yourself. Yet there I was, in the front of the room, about to be prayed over for the one area in my life that gave me joy for the past two years.

I turned around expected the rest of the audience to be standing behind me and was shocked to notice that there were only two other people standing up there with me. Coach Mark started with the young man who was farthest from me.

He began to pray/proclaim that this young man would write incredible songs and that they would inspire and encourage people to worship and that they would impact a generation. It was amazing! I could not wait to hear what Coach Mark would say about my ability to write stories! Then he moved on to the next young man. He started once again and proclaimed that this young man would write wonderful stories that would awaken people's imaginations and stir their hearts back to God! I was mortified! Coach Mark had messed up! He gave this yahoo my spiritual blessing! I was the one who was the storywriter that was supposed to be me awakening imaginations and stirring hearts!

I just stood there shocked as he finished his prayer and began to make his way over to me. Then he placed his hand on my head and started the pray the most ludicrous prayer I had ever heard. He was praying I would give inspiring speeches, that I my words and speech would move people to action and create a transformation in people's lives. The whole time he was praying, I was also praying, apologizing to God about his servant who had messed up. How could have Coach Mark got it so wrong? I guess it was not so wrong; he only missed it by one person. Maybe after the service, I could go talk to the other guy and see if we could switch blessings?

All these thoughts just ran constantly through my head all the way through the coach's amen. As I made my way back to my seat, I thought about how much of a waste of time that had been. Little did I know, that one decision and prayer would lead to one of the most radical and transformational stages of my life, but we won't get to that until the next chapter.

Now it's that time again. I spent all this time setting up just how horrible middle school was, all to teach you this one important lesson—that bad things happen. Sometimes, that is just the way it is, and the way it will continue to be. One of the most prominent questions that people in ministry have to face is, "Why do bad things happen to good people?" My response to that is that it just does.

We live in a fallen world that is far from perfect, and Christians have something called the Blessed Hope. This is basically the belief that there will be a day when those who followed and accepted Christ will be able to get into the presence of God where there will be no more bad things that happen to us. For the previous couple of chapters, I have kept my explanations somewhat simplistic and down to a single overall thought. For this chapter, I would like to explain the purpose of bad things in three distinct explanations.

First of all, bad things happen so we can look forward to the Blessed Hope I just mentioned. The Bible says in Titus 2:11–13, "For the grace of God that brings salvation has appeared to all men.

It teaches us to say 'No' to ungodliness and worldly passions, and to live self-controlled, up-right and godly lives in this present age, while we wait for the *blessed hope*—the glorious appearing of our great God and Savior, Jesus Christ." See? We are waiting for the time for Jesus to reappear to this world, but we still have to deal with the "ungodliness and worldly passions." As frustrating as that may seem, it is just a fact of life. The good news is that there will eventually be a day when this is no longer the case, so we should rejoice in knowing that things will eventually change for eternity. (That means forever, people!)

The second reason I believe bad things happen is to make us better. James 1:2–4 states, "Consider it pure joy, my brothers, whenever you face trials of many kinds, because you know that the testing of your faith develops perseverance. Perseverance must finish its work so that you may be mature and complete, not lacking anything." (Another good verse that makes this point is Romans 5:3–4. Check it out!)

When we are going through trials, it is an opportunity for us to grow and become stronger. Nothing that makes us stronger in life feels good while we are getting stronger.

Working out hurts when you are in the gym, but it makes your body stronger. Studying for a major test can really strain your brain, but it feels really good when you get a good grade. Not buying those shoes you want or that purse or that outfit can be brutal on the teenage psyche, but it feels great knowing that you have the money to help you in the future. So "consider it pure joy" when these things happen because they are good things. They just stink for the time being.

The last reason that I want to share as being a purpose for bad things happening is that they make you appreciate the good things even more. In Romans 8:18, it says, "I consider that our present sufferings are not worth comparing with the glory that will be revealed in us." If there is one thing in my life that is my biggest pet peeve, it is ungratefulness. I listen to teenagers complain that their iPhone is a generation older than their friend or that their shoes are a year older than the newest brand. (But they are also over $100 cheaper! And all the parents said, "Amen!") We as human beings have a hard time appreciating things in life that we take for granted.

I currently live in Port St. Lucie, and whenever I tell people that one of the first things they say is, "Well, you must go to the beach a lot then?" And the truth is that I don't. And the beach is ten minutes from me! There are people who live an hour or more from the beach and go there more often than I do. Why? Because they appreciate it more.

Sometimes, we are going through trials so that we can appreciate the areas in our life that are not difficult. If I was the most popular, cool, most well-dressed kid in middle school, I'm pretty sure I would not have cared for one second what Ms. Wilson thought about my English journal. But because I did not have all those other areas of my life, I appreciated writing a whole lot more, which led to an awesome prayer/proclamation over my life that would lead to an incredible transformation for my life. (Don't worry. You're about to find out about it in the next chapter.)

So when bad things happen, it's okay! Eventually, middle school ended for me, just like this difficult time will end for you. It's amazing how when we are going through a difficult time, things just seem to slow down. Every day feels like an eternity, every moment seems to stand still, just to inflict the most pain in us. I do not want to gloss over this chapter and make it seem like it is the easiest thing in the world to just get over pain, because it's not.

People spend days, weeks, months, and (in my case) years going through pain. Yet I have found that the more difficult the trial, the greater the outcome. Basically, the more difficult the present, the greater the future will be.

Let me take a moment and get real with you. I am not saying that hurt is not something you get over. How do you eat an elephant? One bite at a time! (I am not promoting elephant-eating, neither have I ever eaten an elephant. It's just an old saying.)

As I sit here right now, I am tempted to spend pages trying to convey just how difficult it can be to go through a difficult time when bad things just seem to keep happening to you, but the fact is, I could never fully convey that with these words. The only thing I can say is that I get it. Believe me, I do. When you're going through the storm, it seems like it is never going to end, but it does not go on forever. Just check the weather report. Eventually, the sun will shine again. Hold on to that promise because it is a promise that God gave to you, and His promises are the only ones that are guaranteed to never fail!

4

---⊸◦ↂ◦⊶---

Life Isn't Fair . . . but
It's Still Good

Let's just get the obvious out of the way: that last chapter was heavy. It was, and I considered apologizing about that, but sometimes life is heavy. As a matter of fact, I have a chapter coming up toward the end of the book that actually deals with the idea that life is heavy. (See chapter 12, but not right now. Read the rest of the other chapters first!) With that being said, this chapter lightens up quite a bit but still has some significant weight to it.

So if you need to take a breather after the last chapter before diving into this one, I completely understand. Go ahead and grab a drink of water, or eat something, or watch mindless television, or play mindless video games for about an hour to equalize yourself. It's okay. I'll be right here, waiting when you're done.

Great! You're back, so let's get back to our story. When I last left off, we were trudging through the gulag of middle school with only English class and church as sources of happiness. Nothing really changed throughout the rest of my middle school career. I made it through with decent enough grades and made to my eighth-grade graduation. I was tempted to move on to high school, but I do feel like I need to share one last story from middle school.

It occurred toward the end of eighth grade. Before I go into the story, I must say that the latter eighth grade of middle school was a

40

marginal improvement over the rest of my time there. I finally had the courage to stand up to my father and his (lack of) fashion sense. This allowed me to have a bit of a better wardrobe (the best stuff being "borrowed" from my older brother; without his knowledge. He went to school an hour before I did, so it was easy to take from his closet).

My older brother, Greg, also started practicing his barber skills on my younger brother and I, and it was a bit of an improvement over my father's "side-fades." So with these small, yet significant changes, I began to have a bit of a confidence boost. And it was with this confidence boost I decided to do something I had never done before—ask out a girl. That's right, ladies and gentlemen, the sad sap who you just heard about in the previous chapter decided he was man enough to get himself a girlfriend, so buckle up!

Like any thirteen-year-old boy, I had a crush. And that crush was on . . . anyone close to my age of the opposite sex! Come on, what did you expect? I had no friends and listed five different names of video game girlfriends I had. Even now, I can recall the names of at least six different girls who were blessed enough to receive the affections of young Darred King Williams. And by "receive the affections," I mean that I thought about them and imagined different scenarios in which I saved their life from the unlikely event that our school was taken over by terrorists. And in their gratitude, they each professed their undying love for me. (I told you, I loved stories. Still do, as a matter of fact). Yet by eighth grade, I had honed in my attention and affection for one special young lady—Rebecca (contemplated putting her last name to add emphasis, but it this day and age, with social media and Google searches, last names are just a terrible idea). The main reason I picked this specific young lady was because I believed she was attainable.

Let me explain: I could not go after the most popular girls in school. There was no way I had a shot at them. I also did not want to settle for some girl that I did not feel attracted to (which were very few and far in-between). So I had my sights set on Rebecca. She was attractive, but not in the overbearing, attention-getting way. And her personality was somewhat reserved and introverted, which made her very approachable. We had known each other for two years, but I never had any confidence to do anything about anything (see the previous chapter for reference).

If there is one major thing I learned from my tenure in middle school, it is that gossip and rumors are living organisms. What starts off as a harmless word or thought can evolve into a gigantic monster that can feed off the attention and considerations of any human being willing to give it the time of day. And in the ignorance of youth, there were more than enough teenagers willing to feed the gossip beast at any time of the day. I suppose it was only a matter of time before I became a victim to this raging behemoth.

It is not that I had never been in the rumor mill before; there were plenty of times where John and Jonah (the wardens of my personal penitentiary) had let out various comments regarding my social status or sexual orientation. (They always said I was a loser or that I was gay. Creativity was not within their wheelhouse.) These rumors just never seemed to gain any traction, probably because no one really cared enough about me to really consider this "juicy information" (do people even use juicy as an adjective in that context anymore?). It was still painful enough that I was glad I made the personal decision not to share my adoption with anyone at the school. Yet it would be toward spring break of my eighth-grade year that I would finally get the spotlight.

At the end of every quarter, the students who had made honor roll (those who received only As and Bs) were rewarded by being allowed to attend an ice cream social. (Basically, an opportunity to miss the last class of the day while attempting to make ice cream sundaes out of two tubs of vanilla ice cream, three bottles of chocolate syrup, some sprinkles, and a whipped cream canister that ran out by the third person.)

The thing was that if you had made it to the eighth grade at Roosevelt Middle School, you were probably always on the honor roll. We were a magnet school, meaning that if you did not perform well, you could be removed from whatever program you were in and sent back to the school of your district. So it is at the end of the third nine weeks that I attended said ice cream social, along with everyone else in the eighth grade, because each grade was separated from the other.

Now, I should note that Rebecca's best friend, Stephanie, had somehow found out about my attraction to her introverted friend, but she was kind enough to never let her knowledge extend beyond a sly comment or a knowing glance. Yet for whatever reason, Stephanie decided that this gathering of our class was the opportunity to let go of her inhibitions regarding my emotions. I don't know whom she told first or what prompted her to do it. All I do know is one moment, I was trying to extend the life of my small bowl of vanilla and chocolate syrupy milk, and the next moment, I'm bombarded by at least ten of my classmates encouraging me to ask out Rebecca. It literally happened that quickly!

Let me remind you, that by eighth grade, my status and stature had improved dramatically from the mess on sixth-grade Darred. I was still nowhere ready to handle the weight or status of having a girl-friend. But what could I do? The pressure was right there in my face, and if I did not step up to it, I would have been the laughingstock of eighth grade. And I had worked so hard to move out of that realm.

So I gathered all my personal courage and made my way to seek out my prize—Rebecca. It is interesting to note that while I was in search of Rebecca, one of the most popular girls in school, Heather, actually grabbed me to stop me. I don't know what for. I had a crush on Heather in the sixth grade, but she would have never given me the time of day. If not for this exact moment, I would not even know if she knew I existed. I will get back to that detail at the end of the story.

Finally, I found Rebecca out in the courtyard, right in the mid-dle of the school, surrounded by at least thirty people (no exaggera-tion). I knew I could not back down now; I had developed a follow-ing. (All the boys who encouraged me to ask her out had followed me and seemed to recruit everyone else they encountered.) Just to put it in perspective, I went to a big middle school, our eighth-grade class consisted of a few hundred students, so this was no small endeavor.

So I continued my decided course of action and pushed through the circle of students and walked up to Rebecca (appropriately flanked by a smirking Stephanie) and asked her point blank, "Will you go out with me?"

Rebecca smiled that pretty, yet shy smile, tossed her hair over her left shoulder (Yes, I know which shoulder. This was a big enough deal for me to put in the book, and it's a big enough deal to remember the details.) and stared at me with her light brown eyes and responded with, "No."

That's it. One-word answer. No explanation provided, no apology extended, no pull to the side, or any elaboration whatsoever. It was a response devoid of emotion.

She was not disgusted, or surprised, shocked, amused, bemused, happy, sad, apologetic, excited, flattered, or anything. Just no. How do you respond to that?

Well, I can tell you how I responded. I attempted to play it off. I jumped around the circle (more like skipped around) and kept repeating the phrase, "Okay, cool." That went on until the pain became too unbearable, and I broke through the circle, rushed to the nearest bathroom, and broke down.

I don't know how anyone else reacted, or what anyone else thought. I just knew my life was over, and that there was nothing I could do to recover from it.

Now I know what you are thinking, "Darred, why would you fall for something that was so clearly a setup?" (In case you're not thinking that, let's take a look at the evidence: group of boys egging me on to do something extremely vulnerable, following me around like the Pied Piper, a crowd already developed around my destination, and Heather, who was probably the only person kind enough to attempt to stop it.) And all I can say is I was hopeful. I was hopeful that with all I had endured in middle school, I could achieve something worth gaining and worth bragging about.

So I was naive, and it hurt me. If that were not bad enough, just a few short weeks later, Rebecca would start dating Mark! (Once again, I had to fight the urge to list his last name, you know.) I hated Mark; he was cocky for no reason, obnoxious to no end, and basically the closest thing to anti-Darred I could envision at that time.

The worst part was that Mark was short! Like really short! Now before you get upset because you think I am against the vertically challenged, let me explain. Rebecca was tall for a girl. She was almost the same height as me, and while I was not the tallest in middle school, I was definitely a part of the top tier in height. And Mark was definitely on the shorter end of the spectrum. They did not even look good together! And they dated all the way until the end of the school year!

Every day in science class, I would have to see them with one another, canoodling instead of working (yeah, I said *canoodling*!). It wasn't right, and it wasn't fair! I was a great guy, and even if I wasn't, I was certainly better than Mark!

This would not be the first time I learned this lesson, and it certainly would not be the last. But it is one of the most prominent times I learned the hard lesson that life is not fair! This will always be the case, and it is as true in your life as it is in mine. No matter how you live your life, no matter how you carry yourself or the circumstances you find yourself in, there will just be situations beyond your control where you find yourself on the butt end of a result. And there was nothing you could do to change that outcome.

I wish I could give you some encouragement from that statement, and believe me, I will. But before I do that, I would like to continue on with the story. If I give you all the information and facts right now, you may be tempted to skip the rest of the chapter. But if you did that, you would miss a crucial aspect of this lesson. So please bear with me. I promise it will be worth it.

After my failed attempt to join the dating pool, nothing really significant occurred throughout the rest of my tenure in middle school. It is worth mentioning that John, one of the people who made it his personal mission to torture me for three years, was actually the student council president during our eighth-grade year. This interesting fact will be significant shortly as my attention shifted when I went on to high school. My primary focus was no longer to enter the romantic world but to enter the political realm.

Well, as political as the realm of class politics could be when you are fourteen years old, starting your freshman year, and on the back end of puberty, but clearly not out of the woods yet. (Let me take this time to truly empathize with those of you struggling through the awkward transition of adolescence. I know that it can be terrible and unbearable at times, but I can truly promise you it does get better. For those of you who are thriving with this new phase of your life, don't get cocky! Life gets better, but it does get harder. Nobody wants to peak when they are fifteen! I do not believe that will be the case with you, but extra caution doesn't hurt.)

When eighth grade ended, it was on to the ninth, and it could not have been a more welcome relief for me. A new school meant a new Darred. I was moving on to Lake Worth High School and joining the JROTC program there. (Primarily, it's because my older sister and older brother were a part of it. Why not try to keep the tradition going?) I made a decision that when I made it to high school, things were going to be different, and I was going to be different.

I just did not know how to make that happen, and it was definitely easier said than done. I don't know if you know this, but making friends at a new school is hard—like, really hard. So I did what most insecure ninth graders who have moved on to a new school do, I socialized with the other students from my middle school.

Anyone else see the problem here?

If you don't, allow me to explain: it is pretty hard to reinvent yourself when everyone you socialize with already is familiar with the old you. So the beginning of high school began as a continuation of middle school.

Yet I was determined to be different. I just needed an opportunity to make that a reality. That reality would come in the form of class office.

My homeroom teacher was Ms. Robbins, who taught English (interesting recurring theme coming here), and she was also the advisor for student council. Sometime during the first few weeks of school, Ms. Robbins made the announcement to the class that freshman class elections would be taking place the following week and that each student had an opportunity to run for class office.

I struggle to find the right adjective to describe how I felt when I heard this announcement. It was like a combination of ecstasy, mixed with overwhelming apprehension, tinged with a bit of anxiety, all rolled up in a blanket of crippling fear. That's right, I was afraid of the prospect of running for class office before I even made the decision to do so.

Yet all these emotions did not compare to the one stand out feeling that lingered within me long after those others had faded away. It was an emotion that I had not experienced in so long that I was not even truly sure of what it was when I was feeling it. Looking back on it, that feeling is very identifiable. For the first time in a very long time, I felt hope.

Two days after Ms. Robbins made the announcement, I would go to her and asked for an application to run for office. She was very kind and excited to hear about my interest. She even asked me what office I planned to run for—something I had not even considered yet. And in a panic, I responded with the first title that came to mind—"President?!?!" I blurted.

When I told this story in the past, I have always made it seem like I knew I was destined to run for class president; but no, the decision was made in a moment of panic, not a moment of inspiration. Ms. Robbins must have been well versed in the art of artificial excitement because her reaction was the equivalent of someone who had just been told he or she had won the lottery, not that a student was interested in being class president.

Once again, I must express the magnitude of my class size. My freshman class numbered somewhere around 1,200, so I was essentially running to be the leader of 1,200 students.

Yeah, this guy, not really the leadership stuff of legend you normally read about. Ms. Robbins explained to me the application process and afterward told me the date and time speeches would be given. I froze.

Speeches?

Meaning I had to get up in front of my peers and say words to which they would listen and judge my every word, facial expression, and body language? I did not express my concerns to Ms. Robbins at that moment, but knowing I had to give a speech had pretty much cemented the thought that this was a terrible idea.

I did not immediately back down from the challenge though. I went home that evening and gave myself a pep talk in the mirror. (If you have not tried this tactic, I suggest you do. It really works.) "Darred, remember that you said you wanted to be different. This is your chance and opportunity to make that happen. No one makes fun of the class president; this is the way that you gain the respect of your classmates. This is how your life becomes different, and how you can even make a difference! Don't be scared, just do it!"

The problem was that I was terrible at writing speeches. I mean it! I did three drafts on the first night of what my speech would be, and all of them were horrendous. Adjectives that did not make sense, run-on sentences that did not have a point, and illustrations that had nothing to do with being president!

Writing stories was one thing, but a speech was impossible. It was after my third failed attempt that I realized I was not destined for the glamorous lifestyle of high school political fame (he said sarcastically).

Unfortunately, word of my ambition quickly spread in the group of ten students who had come from my middle school, a group that included my nemesis, John. Remember when I told you John was the student council president of our middle school? Well, he naturally wanted to continue that trend here in high school, so he too had expressed interest in running for class president (albeit, a lot more vocally than I did). I made the mistake of sharing my interest with one of the students from Roosevelt Middle School who had always been somewhat kind to me, and she decided to share this information with the rest of our fellow Roosevelt alumni, including John.

None of the other students seemed to really care about this information, but John seemed to take it extra personally. His immediate response was to ridicule me about how foolish it would be to pursue this course of action. It was soon after that, he decided to change tactics and went about encouraging me to run, claiming it would be amusing entertainment to crash and burn, which would only serve to make his victory that much sweeter. With that being said, the weight of peer pressure once again reared its ugly head in my life and had forced me into another no-win situation. Either choose not to give the speech and be ridiculed relentlessly by John for my cowardice or give the speech and end up being embarrassed and ostracized by the entire freshman class.

I struggled with these options for two days, not seeing a way out. My speech writing skills had not improved, and John's high school education was starting to increase his vocabulary and ability to demean me with it.

So I turned to the only place I could think of—God. That's right, in my desperation, I prayed to God to help me find a way out of this mess. It was about two days before the election day, and I had nothing. So that night, I prayed that God would just help me. I did not give specifics because honestly, I did not have a clue what He could do. Even though, I was going to church, my relationship with God was intermittent at best (*nonexistent* is probably a more accurate description), so for me to pray was truly a move out of desperation.

When I finished praying, I went straight to sleep. Sometime during the middle of the night, I woke up, which was very unusual for me. Anyhow, it was one in the morning, and I could not get back to sleep. It was during this bout of insomnia that I decided to give one last shot at this speech-writing thing. I tried not to overthink it, but just write what I would want to say, what I believed the students would want to hear, but more importantly, what I truly felt.

The result was a five-sentence paragraph that was oddly satisfying in its simplicity. I read it and reread it a few times, not believing that the words on that paper had actually been written by me. Of course, I needed validation that what I wrote was actually worth being spoken, so the very next day, I brought it in to be reviewed by Ms. Robbins. I can remember being ridiculously nervous as I asked her to look over my speech and handing her this piece of paper with less than one hundred words on it. Every muscle in my body was completely tense, anticipating having to fight off the rejection that was about to hit me. You can imagine my surprise when she looked it over and responded with a genuine, "Wow, Darred! This is really good! Looking forward to hearing you share it tomorrow." That was just enough encouragement to give me the strength and motivation I needed.

For the next twenty-four hours that speech became my world. It became the only thing that mattered in my life. I read it, invested in it. I did not just see the words, I felt the words. I heard the inflection, carried the gravitas of each syllable, and pushed through each period with emphasis. I typed it up, highlighted each sentence, and memorized everything about those five sentences that night. This speech was not just something I did; it was part of my being. (Yes, I realize the excessiveness of this emotional tirade, but all you need to do is reread the previous chapter to understand that my self-esteem was at an all-time low before I wrote this speech. So yes, it was that serious.)

The day of elections had come, and for once, I felt ready. I went through the whole day thinking of nothing other than that speech and waiting for the last bell to ring so I could present it. John was also excited for the opportunity to speak and did not waste any time or effort espousing his speech to anyone who would listen. I do not remember the extent of his speech, but I do recall that his opening paragraph explained that he was the class president during his tenure at Roosevelt Middle School, and there were three very desirable traits that made him the perfect representative of the Lake Worth High School Class of 2006. He attempted to goad me into presenting my speech but I resisted. These words were too good to be simply shared during lunchtime. They had only one purpose and were reserved for only the audience it was intended for.

Finally, the bell that ended the day was sounded, and I made my way to Ms. Robbins' classroom, where the elections were to be held. I walked there on my own, equipped only with a piece of paper and a determination that no matter the result, I would walk out of that classroom a different person than the one who walked in.

As I walked in the classroom, the sheer number of the students in the classroom shocked me. There were easily over a hundred students crammed in this classroom meant for forty. Students were sitting in desks, on desks, on the counter, on the floor, and even in one another's laps. I turned to look at the board at the front of the classroom and saw each of the offices listed and the candidates with their names below each office.

Secretary was listed first and only contained two names, the treasurer followed with another two or three names scrawled beneath it, following that was the vice president office that piqued the interest of five contenders. These lists paled in comparison to the *nine* (yeah, that's right!) students who were competing to become the president of our class! John had already written his name by the time I reached the classroom, and he managed to find a seat on the front row. When I entered the room, he issued a pretentious smirk and managed a derisive snort as I walked to the board and wrote my name at the bottom of the list of presidential candidates.

I found a seat toward the back of the classroom, and in a few short minutes, the speeches began. The two secretaries started off proceedings by exclaiming how much they loved the class of 2006, how fast they could record information, and how neat their penmanship was (the main responsibility of the secretary position was writing the notes, or minutes, of class meetings). The treasurer candidates followed up by promoting their prowess of knowing math and adding feeble jokes about how much they loved money. After this came the vice presidential candidates, whose speeches were just about as insignificant and forgettable as the office itself (I joke. I joke. Please do not take this comment personally if you have ever been vice president or currently are vice president of any organization or club, I am sure that your position holds great value, and someday I would love for you to share it with me. Just kidding!). After this, you already know what time it is. (Enter dramatic music here.)

This was the moment that everyone had been waiting for. Let's face it, as necessary as those other positions are, the real competition is in the presidential race. (If you do not believe me, just look at the last national secretary race, or treasurer race, or vice presidential race. Oh wait, you can't because those things don't exist.)

Ms. Robbins announced the first contender, Laura, and the young lady confidently made her way up to the front podium. It was very clear to see right from the start that the other candidates all had a similar strategy—try to get as many of their friends in that room so they could win the literal "popular" vote. It was easy to see which corner of the room was there to support Laura as they cheered her on as she walked up to the front of the classroom. Apparently, this was not the only thing the other candidates had in common with one another as became evident when Laura began her speech.

Once again, I do not remember the specifics, but I do know that Laura's speech contained the following information—her name was Laura, and she was the class president at her middle school, and she was then going to give three reasons why she would make a great class president.

You see, my classmates and I were products of standardized testing, which included writing prompts, and it was during this time that we all learned the basic structure of addressing any writing topic—clearly present your purpose and stance on the topic and then present and elaborate on three reasons, supporting your original purpose, and the nine other candidates took this experience into their speeches to the tee! We all sat in that classroom and listened to nine speeches from previous class presidents who all exemplified some form of commendable traits that made them great leaders.

My five-sentence structure was nothing close to what my other competitors brought forth, which gave me both a profound feeling of relief and terror (very confusing emotions to deal with together, let me assure you). All too quickly, these nine speeches passed, with each candidate being given the appropriate amount of applause from whatever corner of the room their supporters had managed to congregate together.

Then, it was my turn. I made my way up to the podium, ignoring what I am sure was a look of condescension from John. I wiped my sweaty palms on my pant legs and hastily unfolded the paper containing my speech, which I knew I did not need. (It felt as if this speech had been written on my very heart.) I looked out to the crowd once again and made a feeble attempt at a joke (emphasis on feeble), and before I began to speak these words that had consumed me for the past two days, I looked over to Ms. Robbins, who offered me a big smile and two thumbs up.

I looked back at my audience and began to give my speech. It would be impossible for me to give you this speech here word for word because as significant as it was for me during that time, it has been over a decade, and I have simply forgot. But I do remember the general message:

> My name is Darred Williams and I have never been class president or in charge of anything. Yet I do not believe that should be important. I am not here as a member of any middle school but as a class member of the Lake Worth High School Class of 2006 who would like to serve his class to the best of his ability. And that is what I promise to you, that if elected to be your class president, I will do the best that I can to serve you. George Washington once said, "The greatest leaders are those who follow diligently and eventually find themselves in the front, no longer following but being followed." So vote for me, Darred Williams, to be your class president."

The response was completely different from the rest of the candidates; there was no thunderous applause or any cheering whatsoever. I immediately grabbed my paper and made my way out of the classroom. You see, the candidates were not allowed to be in the classroom during the voting, and since I was the last candidate to present, so we had to wait outside.

It was when John exited the classroom that the glass sheet of silence that surrounded me was shattered. He immediately went into this explosive tirade of how asinine my speech was. (I must admit, his language was very "colorful." You have to understand that we were in high school, and as much I wish it were not the case, there seems to be a culture that is still prevailing there that states that cursing enhances your vocabulary. I was as much of a culprit of using this language, as I was a victim to it.) John seem to take particular offense to the fact that I used a quote from George Washington. ("Who uses a $%&#* quote from *&#@! George Washington?!?!") I decided that I would not tell him that the quote was completely made up from me and that if anyone fact checked it, I would be made out to be a terrible fraud.

After the students had voted, they began to exit the classroom, and there was no real change or transformation. One or two students quietly said that I did a good job, but there was nothing significant. Yet personally, I could not have felt better. Regardless of the result, I had accomplished what I had set out to do. I had faced my fears and conquered them.

Ms. Robbins informed all the candidates that the winners would be announced the following day on the intercom during the announcements. That elation I felt lasted about fifteen minutes, only to be replaced by a sense of dread. There was no way I could have possibly won. I did not have my own personal cheering section, and even though I had achieved a personal accomplishment, it did not change my social status in high school.

In a few days, no one would remember my speech, and my life would continue in the insignificance that I had felt in middle school. These are the thoughts that plagued me the rest of that day into my sleep. I woke up the next morning feeling worse than I felt before, simply because nothing changed. I made it to school the next morning, only to find that the only change was John still fuming over the content of my speech.

As I walked into my homeroom class, I looked toward Ms. Robbins to find some sort of revealing expression, but she offered me nothing more than the usual smile and courteous greeting. As I sat in that classroom, the sense of dread and fear increased exponentially. How could I have been so stupid to think that five sentences could completely change people's perception about me? I was still the socially awkward outcast that had plagued the halls of Roosevelt Middle School three years prior. Eventually, the morning announcements came on, and I was 100 percent in my self-loathing.

When the announcer stated that she would now be announcing the freshman class officers, I simply lay with my head down on the table and began to weep. I cannot believe I even wasted any time attempting something so foolhardy. I vowed in that moment that I would never take any more risks and never put myself at the mercy of others ever again.

I could not hear who won each office over the sound of my sobbing, and it was only while trying to catch my breath on one particularly heavy heave that I heard a peculiar noise. It took a moment for me to identify the sound of applause, and even longer for me to peek out of the cocoon of my arms folded on the desk to see that everyone was applauding and looking at me.

I had won. (Let's be honest, did you ever have any doubt? I just spent quite a bit of time setting up this story, how terrible would it be if I did not win!)

You can imagine my embarrassment as I wiped tears from my eyes with my entire English class looking at me, but luckily, I think they assumed they were tears of joy. After class, Ms. Robbins pulled me aside and began to list off the responsibilities that would now be mine as class president. I walked out of that classroom a different person, and from that moment on, my life would never be the same. I will say that even after I won the election, John did not give me any congratulations or any credit whatsoever and continued his tirade of what a pathetic excuse for a human being that I was, but you know what? His words did not sting as much, and with the duties of class president upon me, it made it a whole lot harder to care what one person had to say.

So why tell these stories? Why spend so much time on two very contrasting experiences in my life? Because regardless of how different they are, they both happened to me.

That is the way that life is for everyone. No matter how your life is, you will have your *unfair* share of good and bad experiences. I would hope your life is filled with more good than bad, but that is not always the case.

The only consolation I can offer you is that everyone will have good and bad in their life. Both of these stories carry significant weight in my life, but for very different reasons. The first story made me feel worthless, while the second made me feel valued. Our tendency as humans is to magnify the worthlessness over the value.

Think about it, when someone compliments someone else, it is in most cases nothing more than a passing word. "Her outfit was so cute today!" "That was really nice of him to do that." "I really liked the way that he did that." Yet when we want to complain about someone, we can't seem to give enough details. "Let me tell you exactly what she said that made me angry." "Not only did he do that but let me tell you about what happened last week too." We always seem to have greater opinions about the negative.

One of the greatest things I have learned recently is that our words have power, I mean, I have known it for some time, but for whatever reason, sometimes knowing something does not really mean you *know* something. I promise I will elaborate later on, because this is a huge lesson and I do not want to elaborate on it now and take away from the lesson I am going over right now. It is crazy how someone can have a terrible day that only manages to get worse. Maybe you have heard of the term *self-fulfilling prophecy.*

If you have not, allow me to offer an informal definition. The idea of the self-fulfilling prophecy states that if you believe something is going to be, or someone is going to act a certain way, your mentality and initial interaction can actually cause that expected result to become true.

Let me give you a brief example—if you are walking down the hallway and see a classmate that you are just sure does not like you, you may say to yourself, "Great, there's [insert generic name here], they are just going to completely ignore me and be rude to me." As you pass this person, they say hello to you, and you respond by sucking your teeth and rolling your eyes because you just know this greeting is nothing more than his or her fake attempt to be nice to you. They then respond to your clear aggressive with a passive "Whatever." And you walk away with the confidence in knowing that your original assessment is true and that person hates you. Do you see what I am saying?

I know that is a little blatantly obvious example, but we do it all the time. You know what? If you go somewhere with the intention that it is going to be boring, it probably will be boring. That's because your mentality has created that expectation, and that is how you react to the situation—bored. It is even more likely to happen if you speak these things out loud.

The Bible says in Proverbs 18:21, "The tongue has the power of life and death, and those who love it will eat it's fruit." This basically means that way you say has power, and if you believe what you say you're going to get the consequences from it, regardless of what you say. Now, this is not an absolute—more of an extreme generality.

Just like any rule, there are exceptions. There will be times when you think you are going to have a miserable time at an event and are pleasantly surprised. Or you are really looking forward to something and become somewhat disappointed when it actually comes around. Yet more often than not, you are going receive what you expect. It is that simple.

That being said, I have to repeat once more that when you live life, you have to take the good with the bad.

Life is not fair, but it can still be good.

When you make a decision to find the good in life, you realize that life is still good. I could have moped about being rejected in the eighth grade and decided I could never be good enough to be anything because a girl named Rebecca rejected me, but I did not. Now, did I deal with the class president situation with complete optimism? Absolutely not! Yet I made it through it and gained a great experience from it when it was all over.

The other thing that prevents us from enjoying the good in life is the idea of fairness. This actually is partially not our fault. From the moment most of us are kids we are told things are supposed to be fair. We should all be given the same amount of time on tests, the same amount of food, the same rewards for doing the same amount of work. Can I be honest? This is not how life works; life is not fair. How is it fair that those of us born in the United States are given more opportunities than the vast majority of the rest of the world? It's not.

I could go on and on with various examples of unfairness of life, but I believe you get the point. If you spend your entire life trying to make things fair, you are fighting a losing battle. At the end of the day, trying to make things fair just ends up with people arguing with one another and making ridiculous comparisons that never add up. And comparisons are dangerous, which is why I talk about them in the next chapter.

If you learn nothing else from this chapter, learn this: the bad in your life is only beneficial when you learn from it and move on, while the good in your life only gets better in your life when you enjoy it.

So when something bad happens to you, do not spend time talking about unfair or wrong it was, but take a moment to learn from it. Ask yourself, "What could I learn from this situation so that it does not happen in the future?" When I asked out Rebecca, I learned that you should never follow the persuasion of a group of middle school boys, no matter how many of them there are. (I have taken this lesson with me as a teacher of middle school, and it has saved me from eating many disgusting things, seriously!).

While becoming class president was such a good thing to happen to me, but it was only made better because I enjoyed it. I could have been brought down by the comments that John directed toward me, but I took the time to truly appreciate that achievement. Give more attention to the good than the bad, and it is amazing how the tongue becomes directed to speak more good. And when the tongue speaks good, the speaker receives more good, I guarantee it (more importantly, God guarantees it).

The Abyss

If you remember, at the beginning of this book, I stated that there would be times where I was the bad guy. Up until this point, that may not have been the case, but that is all about to change.

You see, everything up until this point has been what has happened to me as a child. Honestly, there were quite a few things I did that were really bad as a child that I did not highlight at all because they did not add to the narrative or deal with the topic I was covering.

For example, when I was in the second grade, we learned how to write in cursive, and one of my classmates said they simply could not read cursive writing at all. So I decided that it would be really amusing to write him a really mean message, all in cursive so he would not know that it was really mean. (I do not know what I said, but believe me, it was bad!) Unfortunately for me, I was so confident in my cursive ability and his inability to read it that I signed my name to the letter. While he could not read cursive, our teacher definitely could, which is exactly who he took it to in order to get her to interpret. I got in a lot of trouble because of that, and it was deserved. Yet for whatever reason, we are just more forgiving of children, even in instances when they know better.

We have all heard the phrase, "They're just kids being kids," even when the action does not align with what people would deem normal childlike behavior (like forcing younger boys to fight one another in order to receive food—I'm just saying. I've been there).

All that being said, these next few chapters specifically deal with my negative and, in varying degrees, "bad" actions. Not only will it deal with my bad actions, but also my bad thoughts, perceptions, and beliefs. You see, something I have noticed is that many people first believe that God cannot really love them because if He did love them, He would not have allowed all these bad things to happen to them, which is what we dealt with in the previous four chapters.

So hopefully, at this point, you no longer believe that lie. Yet I have come to realize that the next barrier we all must face is ourselves. So many people think they are so terrible, their thoughts are so evil that there is no way God could truly love and accept them. This next section will seek to address that lie. I plan to give you an in-depth look at just how corrupt and ill-willed my mind-set was during my high school and college years so that you can understand it does not matter how bad you think you are, God still loves you! The same way that I know He still loves me.

I once heard a pastor say he would tell anyone in his church anything he ever did, he would even tell his church anything he almost did, but he would never tell his church what he thought about doing because they probably would not come back because of how bad his thoughts were.

This is so true!

Our thoughts are so much worse than our actions, and that is the problem. It is easy to hide our thoughts from other people, but once we understand that God knows just how we are thinking and understands exactly how we feel, we start to believe the lie that He could never love us because they are just so bad. It is the main reason why I struggled so much to write these next few chapters.

It would have been very easy to write about all the bad things I have done, but to write about the bad things I thought? My bad actions are nowhere near as terrible as my bad thoughts, but that is the point.

My hope is that by reading my bad thoughts, you would look at it and say, "If God can look at this man and still love him, God can certainly still love me, even with my bad thoughts." And the great thing about that statement is that He can and still does love you, regardless of any evil thought or desire you may have had in your life. The First Epistle of John 3:20 states, "If our hearts condemn us, we know that God is greater than our hearts, and He knows everything."

That means when you start to feel bad about what is going on inside you, you can know that God is greater than that thought, emotion, or desire. The Bible also states that God is love (1 John 4:8), which means that just as God is greater than our hearts, His love is greater than our hearts! Once I understood this revelation, it made it a whole lot easier to get these chapters started. So with that being said, be prepared because things are about to get a whole lot more . . . interesting (for lack of a more appropriate term).

Oh, and try not to judge me too much. Remember, the whole point I am doing this is in hopes that it helps you out. With that being said, let's dive right in.

5

Motives Matter . . .
but Comparisons Don't

So let us take a quick moment to recap where we are in the story. I am a freshman in high school, and I have just been elected as class president. I had everything I had ever wanted at this stage in my life—a (somewhat limited) powerful position, recognition as someone important, and an exclusive organization to be a part of (hello) student government. In short, my life was looking pretty good at this point. And I was determined to make the most of it.

It is amazing how a little confidence can completely change your perspective on your situation. In my eyes, I was the most popular kid in the ninth grade and the most eligible freshman bachelor at Lake Worth High School. Now was this actually the reality of my situation? Absolutely not! Our freshman class was over 1,200 students, the vast majority of which did not know or even care who their class president was. Regarding my bachelorhood (oddly enough, this is a word, who knew?), there definitely were not any girls knocking down my door to get to me, and who could blame them? Socially awkward was still the definition of my comfort zone, and my not-so-name-brand clothing and connect-the-dots facial acne certainly was not doing me any favors.

With that being said, even though I had made huge strides in personal achievement, I soon found myself returning to the sad state of loneliness and emptiness I had felt prior to the election. I needed to figure out the next thing that I was missing, and that would be my newest mission.

It was at this time that I figured out a new level of influence and ability that I had never really had before—the ability to make friends. You see, up until this point, there were only two types of people in my world—people who cared about me and people who did not care about me at all. Let's just say it really seemed like the second group outrageously outnumbered the first group.

It was during my freshman year that I had an evolution of sorts. I realized that the group of people who cared had seemed to be growing, but it was within that group that I began to notice differences. Some people cared about me because of my position as class president, others cared about me because we were in student government together, and others just seemed to care about me for no real reason whatsoever. It was at this point that I began to think it was not enough to just have these two broad groups defining people around me. If I wanted to be successful in any friendships or relationships, I had to better define people into more appropriate categories to determine how I should interact with different people. (Remember, this is the logic of fourteen-year-old me, so it is a little odd. You will see what I mean very soon.)

So I began to classify each person I encountered at school and at church. (Yes, I was still attending church, but it had taken a *major* back seat to school at this point. I'm talking about the "last-row-at-the-top-of-the-movie-theater" back seat.) Now, to clarify, I did not sit down and make a list of everyone I knew and just wrote them into each category. It was much more subtle than that. I began to just make mental notes of each person I encountered and subliminally put them into one of five categories I created.

The first category was for adults and authority figures. This is easily the most straightforward and direct of the groups, and the most obvious to put members into. Basically, this consisted of my parents, youth pastor, teachers, administrators, etc. Pretty simple, right? Well, even with this category, I managed to split them into two subcategories (Bear with me. I promise I will not overcomplicate this.)—those I liked and those I disliked. To me, this made complete sense.

I knew how I was supposed to act toward those in authority. My parents had raised me right, but the difference in the subcategories became about what I did when that person was not around and what I truly thought of them. To any authority's face, I was perfectly respectful and submissive, but my actions after that completely depended on whether or not I liked them. If I liked the adult, they were safe; but if I did not like them, chances are I had found some way to justify what I did not like about them, and I wanted to make sure that everyone else knew it. I remember spending days mocking teachers, making fun of them in the hallways, miming and making ridiculous and rude gestures behind an administrator's back—all because I thought there was something unlikeable about them.

Now, you may be saying to yourself, "I understand that is bad, but it is not *that* big of a deal!" The problem for me is that I considered myself a leader, a role model, and in charge of the freshman class. When I say that, I do not mean that I just thought I should carry myself that way because of my title as president. I can literally remember times sitting in class, looking at my classmates, thinking to myself, *These kids are so lucky to have an awesome leader like me. Honestly, if the freshman class all acted more like me, we would be the greatest class on earth.* (Yeah, I know. I had a lot of issues.)

In my eyes, authority was given honor by whether or not I thought they deserved it. (Oh, how foolish I was, but we will get to that later. Let's move on to the other categories.) When I look back on it, I realize it is pretty sad that I could be so disrespectful to so many people in this group, because for the most part, I believe they were all interested in helping me and improving my life, but I just did not seem to care.

The second category consisted of "the social pariahs." Now, do not make the same mistake I did when I first heard that term—it's *pariah*, not *piranha*. No, I did not classify people I interacted with as carnivorous fish. A pariah is basically an outcast, and when I encountered these people, I treated them as such. You know what the saddest part of this group is? As I'm writing this, I attempted to think of an individual I treated as a pariah, and I cared so little about them that

I cannot think of one single person I treated this way. I know they were there, but I just did not notice or seem to care about them at all.

Actually, now that I think about it, there is something even sadder. When I was in middle school, I was the epitome of a social pariah, so I knew exactly what that felt like. Rather than empathize with these people and be compassionate toward them, I completely avoided this group.

They could not do anything for me, and if I were seen associating with them, it would completely ruin my self-image and popularity. (Once again, my fourteen-year-old logic at work.) You see, when I put these categories together, I based my relationship off each group on the basis on what they could do for me personally. So of all the groups, I considered these the "throw-aways," but hey, at least they had each other, right? (I really want to take a moment here to elaborate and show how wrong I was, but once again, I want to make sure I cover all the categories first. So please, do not close and "throw away" this book in anger and disgust.)

The third group would have been considered "the useful." They were the people I did not particularly like, but they did have something beneficial to offer to my life. These were the people I treated exactly what the group is called—I used them. For some, they had a video game system or video game that I did not have. For others, they had a relationship with someone else that I wanted to be in relationship with. With this group, I was not opposed to spending time with them, as long as time with them met the conditions I had for using them.

People in this group would ask me to hang out or spend time with them, and it would almost always be followed up by me with some sort of question. "Oh, you want to hang out? Well, do you want to go to your house? We can play the newest Call of Duty? Or something?" (If they chose "or something?" chances are I was not able to make it.) "Oh, you want me to come over? Will you [older, hot] sister be there?" (If she was not, then I was probably "busy.")

This group I considered full of tolerable people. They were not bad people, but they certainly were not my first choice for who I wanted to hang out with on a Saturday night. You know what was the saddest part about this group? The vast majority of them actually seemed genuinely interested in spending time with me and hanging out with me! And I just treated them like things—simply there only for my desired entertainment.

The fourth group is appropriately titled "the wannabes." Funny enough, looking back, I realize that I was a very prominent member of this group. The reason we are called the wannabes is because we wanted to be popular, we wanted to be cool, we wanted to be considered better than the level we considered ourselves on the social ladder. These were my friends. Yes, these were the people I wanted to hang out with because they understood what was truly important—popularity.

So we would spend our time talking about how we could become more popular, making fun of those who were less popular than we were, and basically, just being generally consumed with our self-image. Our lives revolved around what others thought of us and how to better improve that image. Now, I am not knocking people who desire to improve themselves, but there is a huge difference between improving yourself and improving your self-image. We were individuals that were trying to get people to proclaim how *awesome* we were by doing completely *awful* things.

The three previous groups before this were nothing more than stepping stones toward my ascension toward the "perfection of popularity." I would love mocking authority figures in front of my friends to get a laugh, ridiculing a social pariah to receive validation, or bragging about how I had taken advantage of one of the useful in order to show my ability to manipulate others. The fact is that we did not care about anyone, not even each other.

That is what is so sad about this group. We were completely willing to bulldoze another wannabe if it made us look cooler. It did not matter who we hurt, as long as we looked better in the process.

The fifth and final group was what I called "the untouchables." They were the ones that us wannabes strived to be. They were the ones who simply oozed coolness. They never worried what anyone else thought about them because they knew that everyone wanted to be them. In my eyes, these were the top of the high school social ladder. They mostly consisted of your jocks (the good ones, not benchwarmers), the cheerleaders (once again, the good ones), the pretty girls, the handsome guys, and just general people who somehow managed to break through that glass ceiling that I could not even seem to touch.

There were a few untouchables that I truly thought did not deserve to be there, and if I could overthrow them, I could take over that vacant spot they left. That's right, I thought that there was a finite amount of "untouchable spots," and that if I wanted to be a part of that group, I had to replace someone else. As if they had a committee that dictated how many "untouchables" are allowed at each school (kind of like a high-school-popularity Illuminati). Once again, this is fourteen-year-old wisdom at its finest.

Later on in life, when I finally realized the error of this grouping system, I would have the chance to genuinely spend time with a few of the people whom I considered "untouchable" in high school, and I was amazed by just how normal they were. I think the saddest thing about me establishing this group is that they, for the most part, really did not realize how others viewed them. And they really did not seem to care at all. They all hung out with one another because they truly enjoyed one another's company. Now, you can argue with me and say, "Darred, there's no way that is true, and you have just been duped." That may be the case, but as I look back on my high school years, the evidence really does point to the fact that this group spent time together because that's where they were comfortable. Does that mean they never had any ill intentions and truly did care what others thought of them at some point? Probably, maybe, but this is not a book about them. It's about what I thought and tried, so why even speculate?

I know what some of you are thinking right now. You're saying to yourself, *That may have been how he acted and thought of people, but that's not me. I'm a good person, I treat everyone the same.* This would be the moment when I would have to resist the urge to laugh right in your face. The fact is, that is simply not true.

I have come to realize that people say that they treat everyone they encounter the same, but while we may treat people the same, we do not *emphasize* people the same way. Follow me for a moment here. Let us take the simple statement of "Let us go to your house right now." Look what happens when I change the emphasis on certain words in this statement. "Let *us* go to your house right now." This emphasis implies that we want to limit the people going to the house to just whoever "us" is in this scenario. "Let us go to *your* house right now." This emphasis points out that the location is the most important part. "Let us go to your house *right now.*" This iteration clearly shows that the major point is the timing of the departure. I promise I am not trying to give you an English lesson, but to say that the same way we emphasize words, we also emphasize our relationships and interactions with other people.

Think about it. Your best friend whom you have not seen in months shows up at your door, totally unannounced. Imagine your reaction. You would be ecstatic! Now, imagine that your most annoying sibling shows up at your door, or that obnoxious kid in class who just cannot seem to control any of his or her bodily functions—would your still have the same reaction as when it was your best friend?

Now imagine when both of them leave. If it is your best friend, it is a tearful goodbye. If it was your sibling or classmate, you would probably be crying tears of joy as they walked out the door. You see, we emphasize different aspects of our relationships with people. People we enjoy being around, we get excited about; and people we cannot stand, we simply tolerate. Sure, you may let both groups come into your house and accept them and treat them with similar level of hospitality, but you do not emphasize them the same way.

The fact is that we treat them differently because we view them differently. We compare them to one another and assume one is better than the other. The simplest justification of this is that this is just human nature. But what if it does not have to be? What if you could supersede and be better than that? Truth be told, you can! Yet before I get into that, I need to share two different experiences I went through in order for you to completely understand these concepts of motives and comparisons.

The first one took place when I was in the tenth grade. I had been voted class president again for my sophomore year (Yay for reelection!) and was feeling pretty good about my popularity. I had just had my first girlfriend (more on that in a later chapter), and I was rocking it in student government and was still getting pretty decent grades. I had also developed an interest in drama and was a part of the drama club.

One day, we were meeting to prepare for the school year's musical, which was *Fame*. I remember walking into the auditorium, getting ready for auditions. Over in one section of the room, I saw all the students sitting together, laughing, and having a good time together. They were pretty much everyone who I remembered from last year, so we were all pretty familiar with one another, with a few freshmen in the group as well. Then, I looked all the way on the other side of the auditorium, when I noticed a young lady sitting by herself. At first, I thought that was very odd, and I did not recognize her as I began to walk down toward the front of the stage where all my friends were. As I got closer to the front, I began to see the young lady by herself more clearly; and as I did, I realized something—this girl was gorgeous!

She truly was a beautiful young lady, and as I realized this, my destination began to change. I started to make my way over to where this young lady was sitting. In all my bravado and self-confidence, I walked right up to this young lady and introduced myself to her. I found out her name was Barbie (short for Barbara), and she was actually a sophomore who had transferred to our high school from another school. I talked to her for a few minutes and found out quite a bit about her and told her that if she needed help with anything, I was the guy to talk to. She thanked me, and after that, I invited her to come with the rest of the group and I would introduce her to everyone else. She did, and eventually, she became good friends with quite a few of the other students in the drama club. We continued to be friendly toward one another, but it never evolved into anything romantically (though that was not from my lack of trying).

Fast-forward two and a half years later to the end of my senior year, and I am talking to one of my fellow "wannabes," Kris. We had just received our yearbooks and were passing it around to get people to sign it. Barbie had gone from being a shy tenth grader to one of the beautiful girls I considered "the untouchables." She and I had not been really close friends as my chances to date her dwindled down, and I began to pursue other girls. Kris was bragging to me about how many of "the untouchables" (once again, we did not really use these terms, basically, it is just the way I am identifying them here) he had sign his yearbook and stops at the message that Barbie had wrote to him. "I didn't know that you knew Barbie!" he said, with a look of surprise.

I responded that I had met her and talked to her in the past but would not call us friends. Kris then stated that he had talked to her and somehow my name had come up. And when it did, Barbie spent quite a bit of time expresses how much she appreciated me and how kind I was because when she felt lonely when she first came here, I went out of my way to talk to her and make her feel important. I will admit, it took me completely by surprise, but in my "wannabe" arrogance, I brushed it off with some comment about how I could have dated her but it just never worked out.

Later on, I would use this story to explain how one little act can have a huge impact on a person. And in actuality, that is true. Barbie remembered something that I did for her more than two years later, and she really appreciated it. Yet as I look back on it, this really is not a story I should be bragging about or even selling as praise for me because as good as the story of making a new person feeling welcome is, my motives were not right.

I did not go out of my way to talk to Barbie because I cared about her. I did it because she was hot, and I thought that knowing her (and possibly, one day, dating her) would make me look good. I did something good for her so it would benefit me.

Is a good act with bad intentions really a good act? Before you answer that question, I would like to share with you one other experience I had.

The summer between my junior and senior year came with a huge opportunity for me. During my tenure at Lake Worth High School, I was a part of the Air Force Junior ROTC (Reserved Officer Training Corps) program—basically meaning, once a week I had to wear the uniform. I had an ROTC class, and twice a year, we had to do some sort of pointless ceremony that required marching and standing around for a while (literally cannot remember the purpose of any of those ceremonies). This is how I viewed ROTC—another thing to add to my résumé to make me look better.

There was even a time where I almost got kicked out of the ROTC program. I had to meet with the principal, head of the program, along with my parents, and somehow managed to talk myself into staying in the program (by lying through my teeth!). So yeah, needless to say, I did not care about ROTC too much.

On the flip side, there were people that lived ROTC. They made sure their uniforms were perfect. They did the color guard. They prided themselves on being on the drill team. We called them ROTC Nazis (to understand that pronunciation, we did not spell out the letters ROTC, we said it like one whole word, so the two words rhymed and came together—"Rot-c Nazis." I don't know how to better explain it. I hope it makes sense.)

Anyhow, toward the end of junior year, our ROTC teacher announced that our school's program would be participated in Cadet Officer Leadership School that summer and a select few students would be able to travel to the Citadel Military Academy and spend a week there in leadership school. This sounded like a great opportunity for me to add another "thing" (title, position, etc.) to my résumé and, in essence, make me look better. So I signed up and did not get picked (surprise, surprise). Instead, I was told I was an alternate and that if someone selected could not make it, I could fill in for him.

I really did not care about it. I did not really want to go. I just thought it would help me in the future, but I did not really want it to interfere with my great summer plans (work at Friendly's, hanging out with my friends, and just generally finding ways to waste time). Yet my plans would indeed be interrupted as I was called a week before the leadership school would begin and told that one student could not make it, and I could have his place. I weighed my options and believed that it could be beneficial and decided to do it—who knows, maybe Cadet Officer Leadership School has some cute girls there. (It did, but that's not the point.)

So with the help of my parents, I quickly prepared for the trip to South Carolina and was dropped off at the school to begin the drive. I immediately realized my mistake as I stepped out of the car to be greeted by the biggest ROTC Nazis in the school. I am pretty sure they were shocked to see me there, but I was there. We got in the van, packed up all our luggage, and I endured twelve hours of six young men talking about the correct way to shine their shoes, the regulation for how pins are to be put on your ROTC dress, and the correct way to bark marching commands.

I should take a moment and say that there were some benefits to being in ROTC, the class was easy, so it was almost always a guaranteed A. Every year we had the military ball, which was just another excuse for teenagers to get together and inappropriately grind and gyrate on one another. (I still shake my head in disgust for all of the "dancing" I did in high school and college.) And you could get out of class quite often for various ROTC events. None of those things seemed to make up for that terrible drive. I HATED IT!

One thing was brought to my attention during that time that did intrigue me. One of my peers explained that there were awards given at the end of the leadership school, the most prominent being the "cadet of the camp." This was given to the cadet that performed best overall in the all areas of the school. Each and every one of the ROTC Nazis exclaimed how they were going to be the ones who will win this award. Since I was severely outnumbered, I kept my thoughts to myself and secretly thought of how funny it would be if me, an ROTC outcast, managed to outperform them and when the "cadet of the camp" award. It was during that time that I decided that is exactly what I would do. I would work my butt off and destroy these self-pretentious, arrogant snobs by beating them (so that I could be the self-pretentious, arrogant snob over them).

Side-note: I would like to add one piece of information that does not really add anything to the current story but does add something to the overall narrative of this book. During our drive, we did not make it to the Citadel Military Academy the first night, so we spent the night in a motel. While there, all the boys gathered in one room to polish our shoes (*rolls eyes at the tediousness of ROTC).

During that time, we were flipping through the channels and happened across some pornography. This was the first time I had ever come across pornography, and it was in a roomful of guys. It was super awkward for all of us. (How I wish I could have retained that feeling of awkwardness.) We all tried to act like we were cool with it, but it was just weird. I am not just glossing over this fact in order to just brush it off. There is an entire chapter devoted to sex, dating, and relationships coming up. I thought about just waiting until that chapter to bring up this fact, but depending on how much time you spend in between chapters, you may not remember this story when I reference it. So I wanted to make mention of it here, so that it would be easier to recall when I bring it up again later.

We arrived at the Citadel, and they split us all up into different flights (what they call the groups in ROTC). And I was put into Bravo flight. My mission—destroy everyone and win "cadet of the camp." This camp was rigorous; we woke up at 5 AM. We did PT (physical training) each morning, ate only three meals a day, practiced marching for hours, sat in classrooms, and learned . . . "stuff." (I literally cannot remember one single thing I learned at that camp.) We were given a couple of hours of free time each night, but at that point, everyone just wanted to sleep and try to recuperate and prepare for the next day.

Everything was awarded points. Rooms had to be a very specific way. I'm talking about hangars one-inch apart in the closet, each item assigned a specific corner of the drawer, beds made to ridiculous specifications (to this day, if someone mentions "hospital corners," I have to suppress this almost uncontrollable rage). It was so intense that my roommate and I decided to sleep on the cold, concrete barrack floor each night, sharing an extra blanket so we would not have to make our beds each morning. Physical training was awarded points as well, along with marching and team activities. (We made chants to go from place to place and played volleyball.)

After the first day, I was honed in, ready to do whatever it took to become the best. The problem was Bravo Flight was terrible! At the end of the first day, out of ten flights, we were in tenth place, and it was not even close. Half the kids in our flight could not march; the other half were slobs, which meant their rooms were disgusting. We had two leaders of our flight that were there from last year, and they encouraged us at the end of the first day to band together and help one another out. While they gave this speech, I barely listened and was severely critical of their inability to articulate, a motivating message (basically, their speech was crappy and no one cared). So toward the end, I decided to say something. Not because I cared, but because I needed these people to be somewhat decent at what they needed to do to make me look better, so I could win "cadet of the camp." I don't know what I said, but for whatever reason, our flight walked away feeling inspired. We spent that first night's free time helping one another out getting things together. I did not really care. I just wanted them to be better because that would help me look better.

The next morning was an improvement. Throughout the day, our performance was not much better, but the attitude of the flight was phenomenal! During different parts of the day, different members of the group had asked me to speak to the entire group. At the end of the second day, we had moved from tenth place to sixth place (mostly because our chants were so much louder than other groups). By the third day, I knew what my role was in Bravo flight. Before any major competition or activity, the flight would look to me for an encouraging word, and I was happy to oblige. They even started calling me the Pastor. (The irony and prophetic nature of that nickname still makes me laugh out loud to this day!)

My roommate and I started to match up different members of the group to help one another out. We put messy and clean people together to help them keep the rooms orderly. We paired the best marchers with the worst so they could train and improve, and we put loud and quiet people side-by-side so that our chants would be more evenly distributed.

At the end of the third day, our standing increased to 4th place, and by day 4, "cadet of the camp" was the last thing on my mind. Our group was starting to whisper about the possibility of becoming "flight of the camp!" Day four continued our pattern of teamwork and camaraderie, but I really felt like a part of the team on the fifth day. For the physical training, everyone had to run a mile in under ten minutes. The only time we were to be judged and timed on this was the last day, day 5. I had run track and cross-country for two years, so I knew this would not be an issue for me. For some in our group, it was a struggle.

That last day, I gave up any chance to be "cadet of the camp" and ran with the slower members of Bravo flight. I did my best to motivate and encourage them the entire way, and we managed to get all of our Bravo flight members across the finish line with about a minute to spare. But I was nowhere near the front of the pack.

Day 5 was the last day of camp. The following day, we would pack up everything and go to the awards ceremony. On night 4, we were in third place, and we would not find out how much we improved until the awards ceremony. The next morning, we all walked out with our flights and lined up while the ceremony went on. As the ceremony went on, there was a tangible feeling of anxiety in Bravo flight; we had truly given our best. It was especially significant for me. I gave all I had to this flight, and I wanted us to win.

We were excited to find out that our flight commanders (the older kids in charge of us who attended the camp the year before) had won "commanders of the camp." I was particularly proud when it was announced that my roommate had won "cadet of the camp" (partially because it meant none of the guys from my school had won, and partially because he was a genuinely nice guy. ROTC Nazi for sure, but a nice guy nonetheless.)

But those feelings were nothing compared to when they announced that Bravo flight was the "flight of the camp"!

You have to understand, we were attending a juvenile (fake?) military ceremony. You were not allowed to show emotion. Do you know how torturous it is to give this great award to a bunch of teenagers and not let them celebrate until twenty minutes later? After the ceremony, our flight was definitely the most emotional when it came to goodbyes. (And with right reason. Forget the *Mighty Ducks*. Who's making a movie about Bravo flight?)

When I got back in the van, and we began the long drive back to South Florida, none of the other boys in the van said much of anything to me. I did not need them to. I had not accomplished what I set out to do, but I accomplished something greater. I was a part of a team, and I did not need any credit.

Chances are, no one is going to remember who the "cadet of the camp" was at that camp, other than him (I can't even remember his name, and he was my roommate!). But I would like to think that at least a few of those boys and girls in Bravo flight look back on that week and feel that sense of pride. (Maybe a few of still remember "the Pastor," who knows?) Malcolm Forbes is credited with saying, "You can easily judge the character of a man by how he treats those who can do nothing for him." The first time I heard this quote, I was in the eighth grade. It would be almost another four years before I actually had the chance to enact it in my life.

I would like to say that this act changed my life—that I started acting like this all the time and that there are tons of examples of me as a teenager living this way. As much as I wish that was the case, it is just not true. More times than not, my actions were like those of the first story with Barbie, generally good actions with poor motives.

At this point, it would be very easy for me to justify my actions. "But you just don't understand," I would start, "when I was in foster care, no one cared about me, or taught me how to treat people right." But we all know that would be a big pile of crap. (If *crap* is too harsh for you at this point, how did you make it this far in this book? Also, I would like to say I do not normally condone the use of *crap*, but I wanted to make a very strong point of just how ludicrous that excuse is.) The fact is, I knew better. I had spent enough time in church to understand the golden rule of treating others how you wanted to be treated, and if I was treated the way that I treated others in school, I would have been beyond depressed.

When all is said and done, my actions were based off one thing—selfishness. I was selfish and only cared about how things affected me or how they made me look, and because of that, almost every single one of my actions was wrong during this time.

Now I should clarify that it was not my actions that were wrong, but *my motives* that were wrong. During my high school career, my dad introduced a new tactic to his parenting style. Whenever I would do something good and then tell my dad about it, he would immediately respond with, "What are your motives?" For whatever reason, this question just infuriated me! What did it matter what my motives were? Who cares? Apparently, he did. Then he would use this question to justify why I could not do something that I wanted to do.

I would clean up the entire house and then ask my father if I could go hang out with friends on the weekend and he would throw out this unbearable question, to which I would respond with the most popular response of every teenager, "Because." (Yeah, as an adult now, I realize that is the response/word that would infuriate any parent or adult. It just doesn't make any sense!) My father would then turn down my request to go spend time with my friends, and when I yelled at his unfairness with an emphatic, "Why?!?!?!" he would respond with "Because your motives weren't right." What kind of cockamamie (yeah, I said *cockamamie*. No, I don't know what it means.) justification is that? What did my motives matter? The entire house is clean for my parents, and I get to hang out with my friends. It's win-win! Yet looking back on it, I realize that my dad was trying to teach me an important lesson that would take years for me to understand. You see, just like the title of this chapter states, motives matter!

Proverbs 16:2 states, "All a person's ways seem pure to them, but motives are weighed by the Lord." This is the point that my dad was trying to get across to me. My motives may not have been important to any person, but they are definitely important to God. When we get to heaven, we will not be judged by our actions, but by our motives (and to the person that says, "Only God can judge me," believe me, He will and that should terrify you.) Jeremiah 17:10 says, "I, the Lord, search the heart and examine the mind, to reward each person according to their conduct, according to what their deeds deserve." Let me be very clear, when God searches the heart of high school Darred, I will not be earning any rewards because my deeds did not deserve it.

I treated people based on what they could do for me because I was more concerned about my comparison to others than my motives to others. At the end of the day, comparisons just do not matter. No matter how good you think you are, how good-looking you may be, or how talented you are, there will always be someone who is better and someone who is worse.

So why do we spend our lives attempting to get above someone else in a never-ending cycle? Because the world tells us to do so.

We are constantly bombarded with advertising that says that possessions can make us better, entertainment that illustrates that the right relationship improves our status as individuals, and a society that demonstrates that the best thing you can be is better than your neighbor.

I lived my high school career looking at people's potential more than seeing people themselves. The moment an individual did not measure up to the potential I saw in them, whether as a friend, a girl-friend, or any other rung on the social ladder, I ignored them because they were not of any use to me. I have since changed that perspective (thank God!), but only because of a better understanding of God's perspective of me.

What if God only saw me based on my potential? What if Jesus died for me because of what I could potentially do for him? I would be ruined and abandoned by them both! What could I do for God? What could I do for Jesus? Nothing!

Now I know there are some Christians that out there that immediately take up arms against me. "Darred, there is *plenty* that you could do for the kingdom of God! How dare you insinuate to young people that they have nothing to offer God!" While this is true, we are only able to do anything for God through the power of the Holy Spirit and salvation through Jesus Christ. So really, without His help, we really cannot do anything for Him.

I mean, it is like you wanting to help someone paint, but you do not know how to paint. That person then needs to equip you by teaching you to paint and then you can help him or her. So yes, after you are trained, you get to help that person paint, but you also just learned a new skill that you can use now. So I ask you, who is really helping whom?

Yes, I can help the kingdom of God, but only after accepting the gift of Jesus. And with that, I get to spend eternity in heaven, while God gets this broken, shattered vessel that is me. So really, I ask again, who is really helping whom?

Theological arguments aside, your motives matter more than your actions or the comparisons that lead you to make certain actions. So please be better than the high-school me and listen to the advice of my dad. Check your motives. There are so few times that I felt the true joy like what I felt being a part of Bravo flight, and I wish I spent more time in that mind-set than my mind-set most of the time, where I never felt like I was adequate. So if it feels like nobody else cares, remember that God cares. And who could be more important than Him?

6

If at First You Don't Succeed . . . It Doesn't Mean You've Failed

I ended high school on a pretty high note. Things were going pretty well for me by the time I graduated. There were a lot of other things that happened to me throughout my high school career, but I really want to spend this chapter focusing on my mentality and experiences I had during my college career. You see, during high school, my motivations were very clear—I wanted to be popular. I wanted to be accepted, and I wanted to be noticed. Even though I had accomplished quite a bit as a high school student according to the world's standards, ultimately the experience left me feeling unsatisfied. It was during the summer of transition between my senior year and my first year of college that I had an incredible personal epiphany—I cannot find satisfaction by basing my life on what others thought about me, but my focus had to be on how I felt about myself. My goal no longer became about making other people happy, but it was about doing what made me happy.

This sounds great, doesn't it? It is exactly what the world tells us that we are supposed to do—whatever makes you happy. Be you! Do not strive to be like anyone else, only you can be the best version of you. I was determined to become the best person who could possibly be themselves. (Did you catch that? Yeah, I was weird . . . and very competitive. Some people say I still am, but that is up for debate.)

So I spent my summer doing what I wanted to do. I started dating a girl who was a year older than me (which, to me, was a huge deal). She had just finished her first year of college, while I was technically still a high school student. I stayed out late. If I wanted to spend time with friends, I did. If I wanted a day to myself, I kept to myself. Basically, I spent the whole summer doing whatever I wanted, and I was determined to keep the trend going into my college career.

I was accepted by the University of Central Florida (UCF) and started attending college there in the fall of 2006. I was pursuing a degree in political science because the only thing that really captured my interest in high school was student government. (And I was quick to discover that student government is nothing like the *real* government . . . except maybe the maturity level. LOL! Ah . . . political humor.) During my summer of freedom, I realized there were three things that really made me happy—power, money, and sex. (My mentor, Allen Griffin, calls this PMS—the thing that will get any guy or girl in trouble.)

Power to me manifested itself in position. During high school, I was attracted to position, and that was a constant pursuit for me. I felt like I had to be validated by awards and achievements. Apparently, I was not very good at hiding this because I was made fun of for it during our student government's senior sendoff. They took a piece of cardboard and covered it in aluminum foil and wrote on it:

Darred Williams
#1 County Council Treasurer
Thank you for your year
of losing checks, pretending
to plan banquet, and the world's
biggest plaque collection.

So yeah, I liked to have power and loved to be recognized for it.

When it came to money, I was less concerned about the actually possession of money and more about the ability to buy that it gave me. I got my first credit card during my summer of freedom, and it would end up taking me about six years to pay off the $500-credit limit (irresponsible much?). In college, there was one major purchase that was constantly a focus of my friends and I—alcohol. Now before you ask how we got alcohol when we were underage, I don't know. Sometimes we had friends who were at least twenty-one. Other times, people that were selling alcohol just did not care. Come on, you giving a twenty-one-year-old college student the power to give drinks out to people he likes, and he is not going to abuse that? So my money was less about money and more about getting drunk. I know it is a bit of a stretch, but it seemed like alcohol was the currency of my college career. There were plenty of times when we were extended an invitation to hang out with other people, and our immediate first response would be, "Do you have beer?" It had almost become a reflex. So yeah, in college, for me and my friends—alcohol=money.

The last category is sex. Regardless of your own personal convictions, I find it hard to believe that there is anyone out there who could honestly say that sex was not a motivating factor in their life, especially during the ages of eighteen through twenty-two (or twenty-three, twenty-four, twenty-five, etc.). Even Christian young adults have a desire to have sex. Yes, that desire is properly insulated in a desire to get married, but I am pretty sure that it is at least top three in the list of things people looked forward to getting married. Without the restriction of marriage, sex becomes a game, a challenge to see if it can be accomplished. The goal was not to try and find a lasting relationship, but to see if you could find someone to satisfy your carnal desire just for the night. Sure, you had standards, but as the night wore on, the prospect of being with *anyone* sounded better than the prospect of being with *no one*. With that being said, I have devoted the entire next chapter to my perspective and lessons learned about sex, dating, and relationships.

So I would like to spend this chapter focusing on the first two aspects of what would be my eventual fall from grace (and fall I did)—power and money. You have to understand something, as you read the previous chapter you gained very personal insight about my mind-set that people around me did not have. In the eyes of most people around me, I was a really good kid—student council member for four years, JROTC graduate, freshman and sophomore class president, an A–B student, drama club member, and debate team member. Even in the areas that I failed at, people would just wave it off. "He's a good kid. He just made a bad decision." I still wanted to maintain that image, but I did not want my life to be dictated by how others viewed me.

At this point, I would like to make a very bold statement. You can't do whatever you want and be seen as a "good person." Sure, you may be able to hide some things from some people; but I guarantee that when you do something to someone just because you feel like it, chances are, whomever you acted upon will not view you as a good person. Now, maybe that person was insignificant, maybe they were a person you cut in line, maybe they were just someone you bumped into at that party and did not apologize to, maybe they are that boring person in your group of friends who you interrupt because they are so much more boring than you—no matter what, if you do whatever you want whenever you want, you're going to end up hurting someone.

And during this stage of my life, I was less concerned about how others felt and more concerned about how I felt. Because that was just me being me, and if other people did not like it, they were just preventing me from being myself. And that made them the person in the wrong, right?

I started my college career with an organization called LEAD Scholars. This was a great organization for first- and second-year students in college to help them become involved, and it was a great doorway to other organizations on campus. I was really involved in activities with LEAD Scholars (which is not saying much because for the most part if you were a LEAD Scholar, it pretty much meant you were really involved). During my two-year stint in the program, I held a lot of positions and had a lot of titles and gained a lot of experience. It also opened the doors that would lead me to have a role in other organizations at UCF. During my first year, I was one of the leads in our homecoming skit, help choreograph quite a few dances, took five classes a semester (which is more than the normal workload), got a job at Chili's, and managed to keep my GPA above a 3.0. I accomplished all that while maintaining a thriving social life, meaning I spent most of my free time drunk or passed out.

I look at that list of what I did, and it does not seem like much to me. You may feel otherwise, but that's not the point because even with those accomplishments, which some may say is no small feat, that is not what I really remember from my first year in college. What I remember from my first year in college is that I ran for student government, and I lost (who knew that college student governments actually had political parties?). I rushed a fraternity and became a pledge only to be kicked out of it before I became a brother. And I attempted to apply for a leadership position in LEAD Scholars only to not get it, partially because I proclaimed my extracurricular "activities" (getting drunk and such) on AOL Instant Messenger. (This was when Facebook was not that big, and still only for college students and MySpace was on its way out.)

So to anyone looking at my first year from the outside, they would have thought it was a great success. I really had managed to accomplish quite a bit within one year, but I was less concerned about what I accomplished and more distressed about the areas I failed in. This trend would continue throughout my entire time in college. My sophomore year found my becoming the director of the homecoming skit, trainer at Chili's, graduating the LEAD Scholars program, and actually becoming a pretty decent stand-up comedian for a time. (No lie. I was legit. Inappropriate, yes, but still legit.) Yet I still found myself feeling dissatisfied and underwhelmed.

My third year opened up quite a few doors for me. I became the head of the Comedy Committee for the Campus Activities Board. I was in charge of a budget of more than $100,000, and I even played a big role in bringing in Jimmy Fallon to perform at the UCF Arena. I also became a member of the UCF Orientation team. I would spend that entire summer helping incoming freshman and transfer students getting into classes and giving them everything they would need to know to succeed in college. I even ended up joining another fraternity and was a part of a great brotherhood.

These were huge accomplishments, but I found myself more distraught when one of the girls I worked with rejected me. I became depressed because I was not allowed to open for Jimmy Fallon. (Yeah, it would have been a big deal.) I felt destroyed during various orientations because I did not get the chance to be a part of the student success sessions. I was devastated because my brothers did not vote for me to be a chair on one of the committees because they thought I had too many other responsibilities. At the end of that year, my roommates no longer wanted me to live with them. For every high, there was an equal, if not worse, low that I would have to endure.

In case you have not picked up the pattern, senior year was more of the same. I had more than my fair share of successes, but they seemed to pale in comparison to my failures. One specific instance seems to do a great job of exemplifying how the process would unfold. During my senior year, I was a part of the Sigma Nu fraternity and loving life. Each of the sororities would have various competitions between fraternities for various reasons. In most cases, it was to raise money for a nonprofit organization and also helped build up relationships with the fraternities. For the most part, it felt like a popularity contest. No matter how each fraternity performed, it always seemed like the fraternity that had the best relationship with the sorority or the sorority liked the most always seemed to come out on top. I thought about explaining what fraternities and sororities are for those who did not know, but I would suggest you just Google it if you don't know. They would do a better job explaining it than I would.

Anyhow, one of the sororities, Alpha Xi Delta, held a competition each year called Xi Man. There were various parts of the competition that would take place, and each fraternity would have one representative that would compete for the title of Xi Man. In Sigma Nu's past, we had not fared well in these contests, in part because of the "popularity contest" aspect of these competitions. We had a couple of sororities that we really invested most of our time and energy into because we had a good relationship with them, and Alpha Xi Delta was not one of them.

Yet during my senior year, I decided I wanted to change all that. I told the brotherhood I wanted to go all out and be the Xi Man representative for Sigma Nu. I had a Greek little sister in Alpha Xi Delta. (Seriously, look it up if you don't know what I'm talking about. I can't explain every detail. It's just too much.) And I thought

I had a pretty good shot at winning the title. To say I went all out for this competition would be an understatement. I easily spent a couple thousand dollars buying customized teddy bears for *every girl in Alpha Xi Delta*. I stayed up all night one night, baking brownies for their house on Valentine's Day. I made two videos—one for the competition and another about Autism (their nonprofit organization is Autism Speaks), and I managed to raise close to $5,000 for Autism Speaks by getting donations and running for *16 miles nonstop!*

I was in it to win it, and I had the support of my entire Sigma Nu brotherhood behind me. The last night of the competition was a pageant of the Xi Man candidates. You had to put on a skit, answer some questions, wear swimwear, formal wear, etc. My skit was a brilliantly edited video. I had nailed the answers to my questions, bought brand new swim trunks, and a new all-white suit for the dress up parts.

I found out that night that I had raised almost $2,000 more than any other candidate. It was very clear that I had put in more time, effort, and energy than any of the other candidates. You can imagine my shock then when I found out that I "won" second place . . . The Theta Chi candidate had beat me out. For the next year, he would be Xi Man, and I would just be second. That's right, this is not my freshman class speech story. It is actually the exact opposite. When I ran for class president, I did not think I deserved it; but this time, I knew I deserved it. My brothers knew it too, so did many of the Alpha Xi Delta girls, but what could anyone do? You cannot demand a recount for a sorority pageant.

When I was running for Xi Man, my life was perfect. I was working hard and getting things done and pursuing a goal I wanted to achieve. Yet when I lost, none of that mattered. All of the hard work seemed pointless. All the effort of those past few months seemed like a waste of time. This is how success in college was for me. Even when I achieved my goal, the feeling of elation and excitement could only last so long. And then I was back to chasing another goal all over again.

I think the reason why I was so successful in college is because I was never satisfied. Once I accomplished something, after a brief euphoria, I was back to feeling inadequate, insignificant, and inse-cure. The only way to escape these feelings was to chase those other feelings of validation and acceptance. I pursued my power because without power I felt like I was nothing, and I hated that feeling. No matter what title I gained, goal I achieved, or position I held, they never gave me a lasting feeling of satisfaction.

That night after the Xi Man competition, some of my Sigma Nu brothers took me out to eat. They tried really hard to comfort me, in their own unique way. (Basically, they cursed out the girls that we had just spent the past few months praising, which seems so odd in hindsight. After dinner, they decided to take me out drinking to make me feel better. That night, I did not pay for a single drink because the brothers "took care of me."

This brings me to second point of the unholy trifecta—money. (Once again, in this case, alcohol). You see, this was my common response to when power did not satisfy; pursue the next area of satis-faction. For me at that time, this meant drowning my sorrows at the bottom of a bottle (or plastic cup, or bucket, or really any other con-tainer that could hold liquor). I have seen first-hand, secondhand, third-hand, etc., the dangers and negative effects of liquor.

The first time I drank alcohol was when I was sixteen years old. I had just received my driver's license, and my parents had bought me my first car. So I finally had the freedom to do whatever I wanted. Within one week, I was going to the house of a couple of friends (from church, of all places) who were celebrating their twenty-first birthday. (They were twins.) Like every stereotypical twenty-one-year-old living in the world, these two wanted to celebrate their birth-day by consuming as much alcohol as possible. And since I was their "friend," they wanted me to participate in the "festivities." I showed up at the apartment to find about eight or nine people there (more of a gathering than a party). I was the youngest one there, and not being a person to back down from a challenge, I took them up on their offer to take some birthday shots with them. The first time I drank, it was flaming shots of Bacardi 151. I won't waste any time trying to explain to you how alcohol proofs work, but let me just tell you, this is a very high level of alcohol intake. I took three quick shots back-to-back, walked outside, and proceeding to throw up. I came back in, took two more shots, and managed to keep these down. About fifteen minutes after that, I did not really feel any different, so I decided it was time to leave and head to another sweet-sixteen-birthday party for a friend from school.

I do not remember anything about that drive. (Look at me, being an overachiever again, getting drunk, and drinking and driving all together for the first time. Shake my head!) I got to the birthday party, and by this point, I felt great. I thought I was the life of the party—I was telling jokes. I was entertaining everyone. I was super sweet and was generally having a great time. Looking back on it, I realized that I spent the whole evening making a complete fool of myself. The sad part is that at one point during the sweet-sixteen party, some guys were kicked out from trying to bring in alcohol! I left that party thinking I was pretty cool and had achieved a major milestone in my life. This is arguably one of the stupidest thoughts I have ever had in my entire life.

Throughout high school, alcohol was very difficult to come by. I never really actively pursued trying to obtain it, but if it was available wherever I was, I never missed out on an opportunity to partake. I could probably count on my hands the number of times I drank in high school (less than ten!). There were a couple of times with a couple of acquaintances (I really struggle to use the word friend to describe these guys) who invited me over when their parents were out of town where. We drank whatever the parents left behind. I had one friend who had the "cool" mom who allowed her son's friends come over on his eighteenth birthday and drink freely as long as she took our keys from us, which prevented us from driving. (My parents were definitely not aware of this arrangement.) I would drink on a few other occasions; once with a friend at his house and a few times during the summer after my senior year with my older, college girlfriend and her "more mature" college friends. That's about it really.

In college, it was a whole other story. Alcohol and access to alcohol flowed about pretty freely. All you needed was to walk into the right apartment, know the right guy at the door of a bar, or walk into a bar with the right group of people, and you were free to do as you pleased. During my four-year stint of drinking in college, it is impossible to know how many times I was drunk, but I can safely say that it was well over a hundred times (maybe closer to a few hundred, if I am really honest). Would I call myself an alcoholic? Well, during that period of my life, I would say there could certainly be an argument made for it. Yet it did not seem that way. It just seemed like it was a part of the culture. You are talking about off-campus housing where the popular thing to do was line up your empty liquor bottles on top of your cabinets for the entire world to see just how great you and your roommates are at consuming liquor.

Alcohol seemed to be a liberator to me. It removed inhibitions I thought hindered me, when in actuality, those inhibitions were protecting me. I can guarantee that I made a complete fool of myself on multiple occasions at a bar or in an apartment. The only good thing about it was that everyone seemed to be making a fool of themselves. Yet it just seemed like an escape; for however long I could stay drunk, I was free to be whoever I wanted to be. I did not have to worry about the pressures of schoolwork, people's opinions of me, or what failure I had just endured.

The problem was the same as it was when I was pursuing titles and power—that feeling never lasted. I could not stay drunk all the time. (Although there were more than a few occasions where I tried.) I would spend two to four hours consuming as much alcohol as I could to feel as "free" as possible, only to pass out and spend six to twelve hours of the next day trying to recover so that I could do it all over again the following night. My friends and I prided ourselves on our ability to hold our liquor and relished in the opportunity to share each night's escapades with one another, always trying to top the idiocy of one another. For a while, I used to treasure these memories. Now, it is hard not to look back on them in shame and disgust.

You may be wondering why I am so harsh on those feelings and experience, and the answer is quite simply because I was so insecure that the only way that I could feel truly liberated was with the help of "social lubrication." I was so worried about what other people thought of me, that the only time that I felt like I could be myself is when I could use alcohol as an excuse.

If I wanted to dance, and people thought I looked idiotic, I could blame it on the fact that the liquor dulled my senses and reflexes. If a girl at the bar rejected me, I could blame it on the sloppiness of my drunkenness. If I did anything that anyone considered socially unacceptable, I could blame it on the fact that alcohol created a cloud of bad judgment. Drinking did not only become my escape, it became my excuse.

The problem was that I always remembered. And in the few instances when I did black out, my "friends" were sure to remind me of all of my drunken mistakes. I did not like many of the things I did when I was drunk. I simply liked the way they felt. I could not stand going to gross and disgusting college bars. I just enjoyed the synthetic feeling of acceptance I had there. I did not like staying up ridiculously late and going to someone's apartment to drink the night away. I craved the false sense of camaraderie it brought me with my roommates and other friends. I did not want to "hook up" with random girls at bars, but I desired the imitation sense of intimacy and physical gratification that promiscuity gave me.

I longed for authentic acceptance, camaraderie, and intimacy, but I could not find these genuinely. So I created them artificially through the use of alcohol. This is easy to see now in hindsight because of the numerous times while I was drinking when I would break down and just fall into depression. My roommates would see it so often that it would become tiresome to them. They would be irritated when "sad, drunk Darred" would rear his ugly head and beg for "fun, drunk Darred" to replace him.

I cannot speak for anyone else when it comes to understanding motives for things like drinking. I can only tell you how I felt. With all that being said, I do not want you to think I was simply a hurting young man, begging to be loved. That may have actually been the case, but it was not how I acted. I was a jerk when I drank. I thrived on making fun of others and demeaning people I claimed to care about. Yes, it may have been a fake version of me, but it was still a version of me.

I may regret the person I was back then, but during that time, I thrived in that atmosphere. I can remember one time when my parents came to visit my roommates and I during parent's weekend at our apartment—our liquor bottles proudly displayed. All of my roommates' parents supported our social and drinking habits, while I knew my parents detested it. My mother and father managed to hold their tongue, but I would later find out that visit led to a fervent prayer season where my mother asked God to do whatever it took to get me out of that atmosphere.

Looking back, there were plenty of times that God intervened in my life. Unfortunately, I was too foolish to notice the signs. The most memorable of these interventions occurred on July 13, 2007. I was spending time with a friend of mine, and the two of us decided to go out to a college bar and live it up. I was nineteen and apparently, I must have been having a rough week because my friend said that she would use her fake ID to get me drinks all night, and she would take care of the driving.

This was the summer after my freshman year of college, so I was ready to take full advantage of the "free pass" my friend had given me. I spent the next few hours drinking to my heart's content, being the "fun, drunk Darred" that my friends knew and loved. A little after midnight, I began to look for my friend to make sure that my transportation was still intact. I managed to find her passed out in one of the booths in the bar. I laughed it off as I carried her to the car and put her in the passenger seat. I had invited a couple of people to my friend's off-campus apartment, and I was excited to keep the party going. I thought I was fine to drive—the bar was only a few miles from her apartment. What's the worst that could happen (probably the most infamous last words ever!)?

I will not drag this story out as I have done with previous tales. Basically, I was pulled over by a police officer (for speeding and swerving because I dropped my phone while attempting to order a pizza). After a field sobriety test, which I thought I was completely dominating at the time, I was arrested and charged with Driving Under the Influence (DUI) and taken to the Orange County jail. My friend was not in trouble at all because she was not driving at all. I spent that night in jail in what was probably one of the lowest (if not the lowest) places in my life.

I do not think that I could accurately express the full range of emotions as I sat in that holding cell for almost eighteen hours. Let's just say I hit every bad emotion anyone could ever feel (anger, sadness, shame, fear, depression, anxiety, etc.). I was released the next day and thus began the longest process (I would be paying for this mistake for over five years!) of guilt and shame I have ever felt. My parents would not find out about it until two years, after it happened because I worked so hard to hide it from them. (I can still remember the day they called when they found out. It was the only time my father was ever speechless. I'll never forget the shame I felt that day.)

They say that when you get a DUI, it will cost you so much, and they are absolutely right. I spent well over $10,000 on court fees, programs, and stipulations that you are required to go through. I would endure more than a year of Alcoholic Anonymous (AA) meetings, Mothers Against Drunk Driving (MADD) seminars, therapy and counseling classes, probation officer visits, and drug and alcohol safety courses. It was a miracle I was not kick out of college. Had they found out about it, I am sure I would have been expelled from the school immediately.

I wish I could say that this was a turning point for me, that I learned my lesson and changed my ways. Sadly, I just was not that smart at the time. (It would not even be the last time that I drove under the influence!)

I attempted to be more careful with my drinking, but the same lifestyle continued. I was not being gratified with my positions of power, and drinking gave me a false sense of empowerment. I would face another incident a couple of years later, where I was pulled over and given a breathalyzer test right there on the spot. I blew just over the legal limit (and would have been well on my way to DUI #2), but the officers were kind enough to allow me to call a friend and have them pick me up. The following year after that, I was caught in on-campus housing with alcohol and was brought forth to the school's ethics board. I do not think I had ever prayed so hard in my life up until this point. I managed to get off with a warning by the skin of my teeth. As you can see, as I said earlier, I was not that smart during this time in my life. You would think the potential consequences would be enough to deter me from getting myself in the situations over and over again, but in the moment, the consequences just do not seem to exist.

I suppose at this time, I should spend a moment addressing the dangers of drugs as they have an equally negative impact as alcohol does on an individual. Honestly, I tried marijuana a few times, but it never had the control over me that alcohol did. This does not make me any better of a person, simply because our society dictates that alcohol is acceptable, while drugs are not.

They are still motivated by the same false feelings of satisfaction and have similar effects. (This is not about making an argument between the dangers of drugs and alcohol. In my honest opinion, they are both a detriment to individuals and society as a whole.) I was a social smoker. I honestly do not think I spent more than $20 on marijuana in my entire lifetime, while my budget on alcohol easily stretches into the thousands of dollars. To me, drugs and alcohol have different effects but yield the same results.

This marriage of the danger of money and power is not a new concept and should not come as a surprise to anyone. How many times have we heard about some famous celebrity or athlete caught up in drugs or alcohol when they have the entire rest of the world at their fingertips? We sit down and exclaim we do not understand how they could possibly waste all that talent, money, and fame, but is it really such a shock when us "regular people" do the exact same thing? Is there a certain tier or standard to when your life actually becomes too valuable to be wasted? "Oh, if you live in the middle class, it is perfectly acceptable to waste your life getting drunk and high all the time, but the moment you move into the tax bracket that makes you upper middle class, you too valuable to society to squander what you have earned."

We would scoff at anyone who would dare vocalize this outlandish statement, but our actions support this general thinking. A college student who is simply "living the college life" and just there to get a degree is simply in the college "lifestyle" when they drink and smoke, but the college athlete who has the potential to be a professional someday would be wasting their life if they were ever found at a college party with a beer or a bong in his hand. Like I said in the previous chapter, we do not treat people differently. We just *emphasize* different things.

The major themes of this chapter can be summed up by social and self-gratification. I pursued titles so that I looked better in the eyes of others, and I pursued drinking and partying so that I felt better in the perception of myself. Proverbs 12:9 states, "Better to be a nobody and yet have a servant than pretend to be somebody and have no food." Simply stated, it is not about what people think about you, but knowing what you have and who you are.

I was so consumed by looking good in the eyes of the others that it did not become about what I did with the power and titles that I had, as long as I had the power and titles to prove how valuable I truly was. The funny thing was, the more and more I chased after these things, and the less and less valuable I felt. The more stature I gained, the less validated I felt because it truly did not make me look any better in the eyes of others. And if I could not get anyone to notice me with all the fame and acclaim I had gained, then I definitely was not worth anything without them.

Proverbs 23:20–21 states, "Do not join those who drink too much wine or gorge themselves on meat, for drunkards and gluttons become poor and drowsiness clothes them in rags." This is a frighteningly accurate statement. When I drank, I did become poor because I would waste hundreds of dollars buying drinks for strangers in bars or contributing to the "keg fund" in whatever apartment. Not only was I financially poor, but morally poor as well. Morality was less of a standard and more of a distinction between sobriety and drunkenness. (When I was sober I was moral, but when I was drunk, I was not.)

I looked like complete garbage too when I drank and when I was hung over, and all I wanted to do was sleep, instead of being a productive college student, which should have been my main focus. It is no coincidence that the Bible directly addresses the dangers of drunkenness because it is a real clear and present danger in everyone's lives, especially in the lives of young people.

When you pursue these things, you are pursuing a satisfaction that is so temporary that you would be hard-pressed to be able to recall what that feeling was like when it fades away. At this point, I tread into territory where people would accuse me of being a hypocrite. There will be people that read this and say, "Darred, how can you possibly tell someone to not do the things you did? That's wrong." If it is wrong and hypocritical to attempt to save someone from the pain, suffering, and shame that I endured, then I guess I am wrong. And I guess, I am a hypocrite.

But I would rather be accused of being hypocritical than have anyone reading this book become (accurately) portrayed as any of the negative things I became throughout my college career. If me being labeled as a hypocrite helps someone become a better person, and not follow in my broken footsteps, then so be it. I have learned recently that it is not my responsibility to defend myself. All I can do is tell the truth.

Am I saying that you should not try to get positions in school or titles on your school campus? Absolutely not! But if your pursuing titles and commendations to validate your value as a person, I am sorry to tell you, but it just won't work. Sure, for a while it may help, but eventually, you will find yourself at the same place where you need something greater to make yourself feel valued again. It is a never-ending cycle.

Am I saying that you should not drink? That is for you to decide, but I can say with 100 percent confidence that drinking has added absolutely nothing of value to my life. Since I have rededicated my life to the Lord, I have consumed alcohol a few of times, but I have never been drunk since then. There was no real purpose or reason behind drinking those times, and I look back on it and ask myself why I did. But I do not have any good answer. But that is kind of the point.

I still have not succeeded in becoming the man of God want to be, and certainly not the man God wants me to be. But God does not view me as a failure. He still loves me. He still cares for me, and He still continues to work on me. It would be really easy to stop the book right here and just wallow in self-pity and shame because I have failed so many times (and you have seen only a percentage of my failures), but God does not want that from me. And that is not what He wants for you.

Yes, you did not succeed on numerous occasions (just like I did not succeed in resisting these temptations), but you have not failed. God will give you another chance because He wants you to succeed. I like playing games with small children because you want them to win. Anyone who plays with a toddler and tries to beat them is a despicable person, and that's coming from the title-seeking drunkard you just read about. You want the child to win. So you give them extra chances. You let them roll again, and you keep teaching them the game so they can win and get better at it.

God is the same way. If you did not get it this time, do not worry, you will get another chance. It is not failure until you give in to it, until you surrender to it, and God does not want you to do that. For those of you who are worried that I am speaking and extending too much grace, first of all, I cannot extend grace, only God can. And secondly, do not worry, I will soon be addressing what true repentance is all about. I just want to take a moment for people to know they cannot fail God.

He does not stop loving any of us because of what we do. When you mess up, do not think that you have failed God. (That is not possible. That is why He gave us Jesus.) You just have not succeeded yet.

Or maybe you have succeeded in something. When Thomas Edison was inventing the light bulb, he would create over ten thousand prototypes of the light bulb that did not work. A journalist later asked him about how it felt to fail in creating the light bulb more than ten thousand times. Edison would respond with "I have not failed in creating the light bulb ten thousand times, I have simply succeeded in finding ten thousand ways that the light bulb won't work."

I would like to apply that mentality to my relationship with God. I am sure that I have sinned well over ten thousand times in my lifetime, and it would be easy to feel and think I have failed God each and every time I sinned, but I truly believe I have not failed God ten thousand times. I have simply found ten thousand ways that I need to be more dependent on God.

7

You're Not Perfect . . . and You Never Will Be

This is it. This is *the* chapter. If you have been going back and forth as to whether I am a good person or not, this chapter will most certainly push your opinion of me over to the dark side. There will be some people who read this chapter and be repulsed by the terrible things I have done and simply write me off as a terrible person. So before you get to that point, I would like to remind you that me doing terrible things is certainly the message of this book, but me being a terrible person is not the point. This story is not about how bad I have been, but about how great God has been, how great He currently is, and how great He will continue to be. So please bear with me through this chapter because maybe relationships, sex, and intimacy are not the areas you struggle with, but they have certainly been a struggle for me in the past. And I am sure that it is quite the struggle for someone else reading this chapter.

With that being said, I also hope you would humor me for a second as I take a moment to write to my future spouse. I am not currently married, and for quite some time, I seriously considered avoiding this topic because the revelation of my past indiscretions may be too much for my future spouse to bear, but then I was reminded that God's grace is sufficient. And as much as I have fallen short, God is gracious enough to allow me to marry a woman who looks past the broken young man revealed in these next few pages and is able to see the new creation that God has worked and mended to become a man of God who strives to be the best husband possible. So without further adieu, I would like to write a short letter to my future wife, prefacing this chapter:

Hey Beautiful,

Many of the things you are about to read about I have never discussed with you. It is not because I was trying to hide anything from you, or because I was worried how you might take it, but I did not share because they simply do not represent the man whom you know and love. They represent a young man desperate to find you and desperate to be with you; a man so desperate and ignorant that he made a terrible slew of mistakes in hopes of discovering you. I was so caught up with finding the intimacy of a wife that I failed to rest in the intimacy of my Heavenly Father. It is with great regret and remorse that I put down these words and recall how many ways I faltered in my journey and desire for companionship.

How I wish that my story was different, how I long that I could have waited patiently for you, trusting in God, instead of relying on my own flawed judgment, but that is not the case. All I can do now is thank God that He is a merciful God and somehow allowed my mistakes to not rob me of the undeserved blessing that is you. What I have to offer you is far from perfect, but you can rest assured that the man that writes to you now is a man who has a humble heart and has thoroughly repented for the shortcomings about to be expressed and has been refined and purified through God's fire. Nothing I write here can adequately express how thankful I am to have you in my life, so I will not try to do it here, but I will leave you with this promise. I promise to spend the rest of my life dependent on God to lead and direct me, and with that dependence I promise to honor and cherish you as the gift that God has blessed me with.

Sincerely,
Darred

It seems like looking for the right relationship is such a huge part of a young man's life that I wonder if Jesus ever dealt with it. I wonder if Jesus ever had any girlfriends. I wonder if he ever had any girls like him. I wonder if he ever had to deal with any breakups or heartbreaks. The Bible talks about how he dealt with all the temptations of this world, but how did Jesus deal with the women of this world?

I say this facetiously because I am pretty sure that even at a young age, Jesus was more concerned with the business of his Heavenly Father than he was about being physically and socially gratified by having girlfriends. And I think that idea alone can teach us quite a bit about dating. But I am getting way ahead of myself. Before I share my thoughts on dating and relationships, I want to first share my experiences with them.

I should preface this chapter by stating that, like all the other chapters, the things that I am going to share are simply my opinions. Unless I specifically quote the Scripture, please do not take anything that I say as absolute truth. I say this now because I have found that people get quite particular about their perspective on relationships, especially Christians and people in the church. It is interesting that this is such a divisive topic, and it shows just how passionate people are regarding relationships.

I do not claim to be an expert on purity by any means, but I have read quite a bit on the subject. The thing I find so challenging is that it seems like the only way to be an expert on purity is to have been sexually pure for your entire life. Seriously, every author I have ever read who talked about purity was a virgin until they were married. I have not been married, and I am not a virgin (I do not say that with pride, but I also do not say it with shame. I simply state it to be completely transparent and honest.), so it seems to me I would automatically be exempt from the possibility of being pure ever again. Or so I thought for the longest time.

As I have grown and matured, I have come to realize that purity is about so much more than just sexual intercourse. Don't get me wrong, sex plays a huge role in it, but I have seen plenty of young people who prided themselves on being virgins, yet they had no qualms being a part of any other sexual act as long as it was not explicit *sex*. At the same time, I have seen people who have had a past of sexual addiction or still struggle with the temptation, but something about them just exudes a sense and desire to be pure. I don't know if I could say this chapter is specifically about purity, but I will certainly do my best to address it.

One last disclaimer before I begin. In the previous chapters, I have been pretty open and honest with the different characters in my stories, but I will not be as open or forthcoming with the young women in this chapter. This is not an attempt to hide any information from you, but to simply protect the identity and integrity of the women I have known and been in relationships with. This is my story to tell, and it is not my place to divulge their personal information in any way. So if the tone seems more reserved than previous chapters, that is the reason for it. Let's get started.

The first time a girl actually expressed interest in me was in the fourth grade. The young lady put a handmade card in my desk, which boldly expressed in large, block letters, "Darred, I love you, baby!" I didn't know what to do with it, so I threw it away and pretended like I never received it. The first time I held hands with a girl was when I was twelve years old, with my first "summer love" that I met while on family vacation at a time-share in Arkansas.

The first time I kissed a girl was when I was thirteen, and it was when I was playing truth or dare with some friends. It would be another two years before I would kiss again, and that time, I was playing spin the bottle with some classmates at a school party. Needless to say, I do not have the magical tale of a wonderful first kiss. Maybe this callousness to what many would consider a romantic milestone explains my generally cavalier attitude toward relationships when I was young, but there's no way for me to know for sure.

It would not be until my sophomore year of high school that I would get my first girlfriend. I met her during the homecoming dance, and I thought she was somewhat attractive, but certainly not drop-dead gorgeous. (I now recognize the beauty of all of God's daughters. I am simply trying to give you some insight into my juvenile mind.) After the dance, I began to notice this young lady more and more. It seemed like she was now in places she had never been before: at my lunch table, in front of my classes, and by my locker.

Let me remind you that two years before this, I had my heart crushed by a young lady at an ice cream social, in what was expressed to me as a "sure thing," so I was very hesitant to act on what you may view as "obvious interest." After a couple of weeks of consistent interaction, I decided to act on it and ask her out. She said yes and seemed overjoyed. (Literally, as I walked away, I heard her scream right behind me.) Thus, would begin my first official girlfriend-boyfriend relationship.

What followed were three weeks of what I deemed the "routine relationship." I would get to school in the morning, find my girlfriend and her friends, sit around and listen to the latest gossip, walk her to class, give a little "pop" kiss, and then run to my class to make sure I did not get there late. After class, I would meet her at her locker, carry her books, walk her to the next class, and sprint toward mine, once again in an effort not to be tardy. In that three-week period, we never went on any dates. I never talked to her on the phone, and there never seemed to be any substantial or intimate conversations that we had with one another. The only real benefit I saw from the relationship was that I got to get a peck kiss after each period, and everyone seemed to look at me differently because I had a girlfriend.

At the end of three weeks, I decided that the pros did not outweigh the cons, and I decided to break up with her. I made the decision on a Friday but decided to wait to give her the news until Monday, so that I would not ruin her weekend by feeling miserable about losing me. That afternoon, I walked her to the front of the school where the parents picked up their children, so she gave me the obligatory "pop" kiss along with note for me, folded up "origami-style (seriously, how do girls learn how to fold those crazy things?). I waited until I got on the bus before I read it, and come to find out, and she *broke up with me* in that note!

First of all, who breaks up with someone with a note? Second, how dare she break up with me when I had already decided to break up with her! My anger subsided by the time I made it home that afternoon, and I had a pretty good weekend. The following Monday, neither one of us talked to the other. No one else brought it up, and we moved on. I thought I had successfully navigated my first real relationship.

It would be another year before I dated another girl, oddly enough. I met her the same way I had met my first girlfriend, at the homecoming dance. At this point, I had quite a bit more experience when it came to being attracted to the opposite sex—primarily with the help of my "summer loves." (*Grease* really knew what it was talking about when they put together that song #feelingold.) Basically, every summer my parents would take us to some time-share in a different part of the country, and in each location, I managed to find at least one moderately attractive young woman to spend the week with. (I actually have no reservations sharing the names of those young ladies, considering I can't remember their last names, and they are spread all across the country—Amanda in Arkansas, Tracy at Myrtle Beach, Caroline in Arizona, Nikki at Hilton Head Island, and Nicole in Orlando.) There were also few other young ladies in my high school that showed me some attention that I reciprocated, but it never man-ifested into an actual relationship.

Anyhow, I started dating this girl (I was a junior and she was a sophomore), and this relationship added a few more layers to the dynamic. We would talk to each other on the phone at night. I would go visit her and hang out at her house, spend time with her friends outside of school, and actually meet her parents. Along with these additions, there were physical aspects as well. We would make out, and our hands would roam over one another, never underneath the clothing, but enough to add to a sexual desire.

That relationship would last a few months before she broke things off with me, once again, with a note! (Have some courage ladies!) This one actually had quite a bit more of an impact on me. I remember going to her house and asking for an explanation, which she never gave. Rather than taking a moment to recuperate, I decided to dive right back into the dating pool in the worst way possible. Let me explain.

While trying to find an explanation and sitting beside this girl right after she broke up with me, I recalled that one of her friends confessed to her that she thought I was pretty cute. Once I had seen there was no possible way that the two of us were not going to get together, I asked her if I could have the phone number of the girl who expressed her attraction to me. (Yeah, I know, that's bad.) The crazy thing is that she said okay, and that night, I was at the movies with a new girl!

This young lady would be my third official girlfriend, and once again, the concept of dating relationship evolved for me once again. This time, the evolution was primarily physical. Making out no longer seemed to satisfy me, and now it was not enough to allow my hands to roam, but articles of clothing had to be discarded at times. We never got close to any sort of sexual acts, but we imitated it quite a bit. This was also when I started to let a relationship supersede my other responsibilities.

I don't remember a lot of the reasons why, but I do remember there were more than a few times when I lost my driving privileges because of my relationship with this girl. Once again, this relationship ended up with her breaking up with me. (Anyone seeing a trend here?) And for the first time, I can remember me actually taking a break up pretty hard. I cried for quite a bit, and there were more than a few awkward moments of showing up at her house unannounced. (Just don't do it, gentlemen. It's not as romantic as the movies make it out to be.) But somehow, I eventually got over it.

I would eventually have one more girlfriend during my tenure in high school, but before I get to that, there is another couple of quick events that occurred before that. After that girl, I did not date anyone until my senior year. At the beginning of my senior year, I would start hanging out with some "friends" that were basically my friends because they had the most freedom and access to alcohol. Normally, it was just three guys sitting in an empty house, drinking and being idiotic.

Yet there was one specific occasion where one of the friends invited three girls to join us. The ringleader of our group was interested in one of the girls, and she brought some friends to hang out with. I ended up making out with one of the girls and just enjoying being validated by getting attention.

The very next night, my "friend" invited us to hang out again and told us that the girls would be joining us again. Before the girls got there, my "friend" gave me a condom, and not wanted to seem socially unacceptable, I took it and probably made some lewd comment about what I was going to do to that girl that night. (My stomach turns just thinking about it.) The girls showed up, but there were only two this time, the ringleader of the girls and the girl I had made out with the night before.

When everyone else passed out, me and the girl made our way to my friend's little brother's room and had sex. Yeah, that's how I lost my virginity. Not to the love of my life. There was no Usher or Ne-yo (I may be dating myself here.) playing in the background. I had known the girl less than forty-eight hours, and here we were, not sure how to move on from what I could only describe as the most awkward situation ever.

Why did I do it? If I am truly honest, it is because it felt good, and she was willing. I know that sounds terrible, but it is the truth. Part of me also thought that it would make look better in the eyes of other young men. Maybe it did—I don't know. I simply can't remember. The sad part is that a few short weeks later, my "friend" would invite the ringleader of the girls over again, and this time she came with a different girl. And somehow I managed to have sex with that girl too. (I say "managed" because I don't know how I could convince a girl I met that night to have sex with me.)

When this first happened, I thought to myself that this girl has some very promiscuous friends, when in fact, I am sure everyone else had to have thought I was the promiscuous one. Isn't that how it always is? Society says that a girl who sleeps around is a "slut," while a guy who does the same thing is called a player. I expected to be praised for something I expected should make those girls ashamed of themselves. There is no explanation or justification to this; I am simply sharing the facts.

My senior year was a "liberation" of sorts for me. I would date one more girl, a young lady from the church I attended, but I was less concerned with the dating aspect and much more concerned with physical aspect. This young lady was a virgin, and I was not. So I thought I was "respecting" her by not forcing sex upon her. Instead, we managed to do everything but sex, including stripping of clothing and oral sex. We would go to a park in the evening and spend time together in my car. There were even a few times where I would pick her up from church and take her out there. As the physical connection grew, I became more emotionally detached. We hardly talked (who had time to talk when sexual gratification was possible?), and she would constantly accuse me of being distant and not invested in the relationship.

As a matter of fact, this would be the first and only time I would ever cheat on a girlfriend. I completely understand how a man could be led to cheat—when a relationship is only about sexual gratification, you care very little who it is satisfying that need. Since my girlfriend was from church, I thought it would be perfectly acceptable to pursue a girl I went to school with, and we made out with each other.

Luckily, she found out about my girlfriend almost immediately after the incident and instantly distanced herself from me. (I didn't think it was lucky at the time, but I am thankful that was not a habit I picked up.) Eventually, my fourth and final high school girlfriend would break up with me, but unlike the previous ones, the breakup had very little impact on me. Breaking up with her simply afforded me more opportunities to find new sexual partners.

I would date one other girl during the summer after my senior year. She had just finished her first year of college, so I was excited and proud of the fact that I was dating an "older woman." In fact, technically I was still high school student and she was in college, so that earned me quite a bit of admiration from my friends. This would be my first committed relationship where I would have sex consistently with my significant other. It was also the first time that I started to have conflicting feelings regarding relationships.

After the summer, I would head to the University of Central Florida, while she was going to Florida State University. So we attempted to have a long-distance relationship, and it worked for a few months. We would travel to visit each other every two weeks. I would go see her in Tallahassee, and two weeks later, she would come visit me in Orlando. It seemed like a good system. Yet as we became more familiar with one another, I realized that some of our views just did not really match up.

This came to a head one weekend when I went to visit her and attended a house party with some of her friends. I was shocked to find pornography playing on the big screen television, while the apartment was packed with people. This was not my first encounter with pornography, but I had always viewed it as something to be indulged in private, to see it so flippantly presented just made me feel quite uncomfortable. The oddest part was that it did not seem to affect anyone else at the party. I remember sitting there for quite some time, playing solitaire, until finally I just could not handle the atmosphere and walked out.

My girlfriend at the time would come after me later, and we talked about how things just did not seem to fit anymore. I am not sure what the exact reason was, but for whatever reason, we broke up that night. I was emotionally devastated but still felt oddly relieved. Many people would say it was the conviction of the Lord that compelled me to do that, but I do not want to make myself out to be that self-righteous. I was not serving the Lord at that point. I was not even going to church at the time. That is not to say that God cannot work in the lives of those who are not serving Him. I just want to make it abundantly clear that if that was the Holy Spirit working in me, then it was 100 percent Him at work because I did nothing to make that happen on my own.

From this point on, my relationship/sex life throughout college would be majorly conflicted, but not in the same way as with my long-distance relationship. Looking back on it, I realize that somewhere along the line, I had subliminally categorized girls the same way that I had done with people when I was in high school. This time, I put all girls into three distinct categories.

The first category was the "one-night-stands." These were the girls whom I did not necessarily view as overly attractive or very interesting, but they were girls who could help me satisfy my sexual urges. The combination of the bar atmosphere and alcohol allowed me the chance to get with one of these young ladies every few months. I would wake up the following morning with feelings of remorse, regret, and immediately planning on how to escape to avoid any sort of awkward "morning-after" exchange. I had very little consideration for these young women, and it breaks my heart to look back and know I was ever that type of person.

The second group was the "hook-ups." These girls were very similar to the first category, but the major difference was that I wanted to brag about these encounters. These were young women I thought were physically attractive but had something I would wrongly equate as a "fatal flaw"—their voice was too annoying, they were too clingy, they were not that intelligent, or they were just boring. Basically, I viewed these girls as good enough to "hook up" or "fool around" with, but because of whatever small flaw they carried, I did not deem them good enough to date or consider a serious relationship with them. I would not consider a serious relationship, but I did not mind bragging to my friends that I had spent the night with them. These were probably a bit more infrequent than the first group, but still managed to be present.

The third and final category of girls would be the "potential suitors." These were girls that were girlfriend material. They were the ones I wanted to go after—girls who were worth pursuing—and pursue them, I did. Throughout my four years in college, I probably encountered four or five of these girls, at least encountered enough to the extent to actually pursue them. A few of them gave me the time of day; others did not think I was worth it.

It is funny, looking back on it. I realize that many of the girls I viewed as "potential suitors" treated me the same way I treated the girls that viewed as "one-night stands" and "hook-ups." It is very interesting when you become treated the way you treat others and you find yourself not liking it. I hated the feeling of these young ladies not viewing me as good enough, without even considering for a second the young ladies I had treated that same exact way.

A few of the girls I viewed in the third group would actually spend a night with me, only to push me away the following morning. I could not understand this flip of intimacy hierarchy, even though I had become a member of this new society. The society I am talking about is the one that does intimacy backwards.

When we learn about intimacy as teenagers, we are taught that first you date, then you kiss, and you slowly progress, and are very careful who you become physically intimate with, eventually treasuring your virginity until the perfect person comes along that you wish to give that gift to. (Granted, this is not how I went about it, but it was what I was taught.) In college, it seemed like that progression was flipped. Young people seemed willing to give physical intimacy to whoever they wanted, having sex with whoever you felt like, only to be more selective about who you would go out went, and then treasuring the coveted title of boyfriend/girlfriend and holding out for that perfect person to fill that role for us.

This seems like a major fallacy in our society today. People seem to value things that are so much more trivial, and place very little value in things that should be cherished. That being said, I believe there is still an innate God-given feeling of cherishment and value.

Allow me a moment to explain: one of the girls I considered a "potential suitor" allowed me the chance to take her out. We had dinner and ended up back at her place. That night, we ended up having sex; and in my carnal mind, I thought the night went great. As I tried to follow up with her the following days, she completely ignored me, eventually coming out and stating I did not value her. I was astonished. This girl had invited me into her home, and she and I had both mutually consented to sex. (There had not even been alcohol involved.) So how could she demand that I value her sexuality when it seemed like she did not value it herself?

Looking back, I have come to realize that God has placed an innate desire within women to be treated valuably, even if they do not value themselves. It is the responsibility of the man to protect a woman, and it is the responsibility of a woman to hold a man to that responsibility. When it comes to dating and sex, I truly believe that it is up to the man to set the standard, and the woman helps guide and correct the man to hold fast to the standards that he has established. There are a lot of verses about sexual immorality and relationships in the Bible, but I believe that one simple concept can truly set up couples for dating success. Matthew 7:12 states, "So in everything, do to others what you would have them do to you, for this sums up the Law and the Prophets."

If you treat your girlfriend or boyfriend the way that you would want your future spouse to be treated, you can truly do no wrong. If we are truly honest, none of us want our spouse to have ever been one who was ever considered promiscuous. Yet we have no problem reveling in sexual promiscuity and expecting our future spouse to simply be accepting and forgiving of our previous transgressions.

This is not a right mind-set. Everyone is looking for "the one," but very few have focused their intentions on *becoming* "the one." My heart breaks every time I think about my sexual exploits and how they may negatively affect my marriage. Yet even dwelling on that can be a misstep. You see, this is normally the end of those books on purity, the part where you close it and feel like the worst sinner in the world. In the past, I would end up walking around in a shame spiral for the next few weeks, until eventually I forget about it until the next book comes along, or the next sermon on purity shows up, and I crash and repeat the process all over again.

That is why the Bible is so important because it gives us the next step and a way to resist shame. The First Epistle of John 1:8–9 tells us, "If we claim to be without sin, we deceive ourselves and the truth is not in us. If we confess our sins, he is faithful and just and will forgive us our sins and purify us from all unrighteousness." Did you catch that? He will *purify* us, meaning that there is a way to be pure after sin. All it takes for us to do is confess our sins.

Now, here is the kicker, we do not just go back to sinning and sleeping around like we did in our past. If you are arrested for committing a crime, and you confess to that crime, and the judge allows you to go free, it is not expected for you to go out and commit the crime again. If you continue to do the same wrong thing, you will eventually have to face consequences for it. For sex, sometimes it comes in the form of something physical—things like pregnancy or sexually transmitted diseases. For me, the consequences of my sexual indiscretions came in the form of emotional distress.

Let's get one thing straight regarding my "sexual liberation" in college, the vast majority of the time I did not enjoy it. Sure, the act of sex feels good (anybody who tells you otherwise is either lying or not doing it right), but that was a few minutes of gratification, which would then be followed up with days of loneliness or depression.

You can ask my college roommates and friends. I spent more nights depressed and alone than I did with a girl in my bed. It was because I was seeking out something right and only getting something wrong instead. My entire being craved true intimacy, but I only knew how to search for an artificial companionship that did not to satisfy this incredible desire I had within me.

I was tempted to just stop there, but I hate it when authors, pastors, and leaders sum up their pain and suffering of a difficult season in just a few short sentences. It does not give true weight to what they really went through. I know that I cannot accurately convey just how challenging the time was and how sinful I was in words written on a page. I could write a whole other book on that topic alone and still not fully convey how terrible it was, but I want to make sure I do my best to emphasize it now. The problem is that I did not know what I was looking for. I was attempting to be fully satisfied from the admiration and love of an individual girl, and that is impossible. And then whenever they rejected me, I felt completely worthless because I placed so much emphasis on their opinion.

I know for a fact there are some who are in this lifestyle who know that this is not an easy thing to walk away from, and you are correct. It was not easy for me. God had to literally isolate me from everyone around me who had lived that lifestyle with me. I did not make this change. I did not stop it. I did not know how to stop it, and it took God to transform me. He wants to help, and He will help if we ask for it. But it takes time.

When I made a decision to serve the Lord, He helped me by removing the vast majority of distractions. That does not mean it was a perfect road. I apologetically admit that even after rededicating my life to the Lord, I messed up and had sex on a few occasions. But the circumstances were much different. I was not actively pursuing sexual intercourse and it was harder for me to have sex than it was in the past.

No matter what I do, my past mind-sets and struggles still affect me, which is why I need to constantly go to Jesus. Just recently, there was a young lady that I was "pursuing" ("talking to," "pre-dating," whatever nonsensical term you want to use. The term we settled on was "getting to know each other."), and she basically cut the relationship short. It does not matter why. All that matters is that it happened. I was devastated, and I did not know how to handle it.

For all the areas God had worked in me, this was an area I was still weak in. I walked around for weeks, thinking that I was worthless, and this is *after* understanding the truth of God's love for me. God was faithful during this process though. He has picked me up and fixed the broken pieces of my heart, but I still have moments of weakness. I get past most of them, but there have been one or two occasions that have let the emotions lead to bad decisions (not sexual "bad decisions," but even as a Christian, I have still had my fair share of regrettable texts and phone calls).

My fear is now that young lady has lost any respect or admiration she had for me before. Yet even that is a flawed logic. My goal is not to impress or seek the approval of any man or woman, but to seek the approval of God. This is because when we seek God's approval, He makes us whole (which is similar to the term *holy*), and those who are looking to God will notice that their heart is pursuing God as well. And that will give them a level of respect and admiration that surpasses anything they can show off or create on their own.

Allow me a moment to give some encouragement to the young Christian man striving to get married. Seek God and His will. That will make you ridiculously attractive to women seeking after God (like really, really ridiculously attractive). Believe me, I know this is hard. Even as I write this, I'm thinking that I could never do this without wondering why that girl does not notice me. But if there is a girl you are interested in who is not impressed with your pursuit of God, then maybe she is not pursuing God the way you would want your future wife to be pursuing Him.

If the young woman truly is pursuing God, there is nothing more unattractive to her than a man who pursues her more than he pursues God. (Take my word for it!) That is my biggest regret when it comes to any of my Christian relationships. Many times, I pursued the woman I wanted to spend the rest of my life with more than I pursued the God that I would spend eternity with. Don't make the same mistake I did.

The transformation that God makes within us is far from perfect, not because He is imperfect, but because we are. The moment we attain perfection is the moment we no longer need God, and as long as we live in this world, we will need God. So do not get discouraged when you fall short, when you fail, when you mess up, or when you make a mistake. Just go back to Him and confess your sins and allow Him to purify you.

When I was not committed to God, it was really easy to sin and really hard to do the right thing. Now that I am in a committed relationship with Him, it is a lot harder to sin but much easier to do what is right. That does not mean I never do anything wrong and I always do what is right. I am far from perfect, but I am certainly moving in the right direction.

8

You're a Story, Not a Statistic

So do you hate me yet? Do you think I am a despicable person? If you do, that is quite all right. I do not really like the guy I have been writing about for these past few chapters either. As a matter of fact, part of me began to question why anyone would like this guy at all? I mean, seriously, knowing what you know about me now, would you really want to be friends with me?

All the Christians reading this are responding with grace and love, thinking about how they would befriend me, in order to lead me to Jesus, and I thank you for that. All the unsaved guys are thinking that I would be really cool to hang out with but really would not trust me for anything really important in their lives. All the girls/ young women (Christian or otherwise) would not want to have anything to do with me, *at all*! Yet I did have to take a moment and think about how I had any friendships and relationships at all during this time.

The answer to that is very simple: I hid the truth from people. It would have been very difficult to make friends if I was 100 percent honest with them from the get-go. Could you imagine an eighteen-year-old Darred Williams walking up to you and saying, "Hey, I don't value you as a person, but I like all the stuff you have. Can I come over to your house and use your stuff and never really talk to you or spend any significant amount of time with you?" Or having me walk up to college girl at a bar, "Hey, I have no interest in you as a person, but I would like to use you for your body and have sex with you tonight?" (Sadly, this seems like a much more common occurrence and socially appropriate approach in bars nowadays.) Nobody would want to be friends with that person. Nobody would trust him either. So I did what any individual who wants to have his or her way, but refuses to change for the better—I lied and pretended like I was better than I really was.

We have all done it (except for you, of course. This is just for the other 6,999,999,999 people on earth). We pretend to be someone we are not to get something we want. I actually remember one time I pretended to be a vegetarian to impress some girl who was a vegan (thought about telling her I was vegan also, but it was just too much). I would call classmates in high school my "best friends" just so they would invite me over to their house and play their video games.

I did a lot because I had ulterior motives. How did I justify these actions? By playing the old "I'm still a good person" card, or the even more popular, "At least I'm not as bad as [enter the name of generic terrible person you know here]." This is generally how people cope with the bad things they do, they *statistisize . . . statisfy . . .* (← When you attempt to make up a new word, and it makes no sense.) They basically use statistics to justify their actions. If I am better this much of the time, it makes up for the rest of the time when I'm terrible—that was my logic.

Can we really blame people for thinking this way? We use statistics to justify just about everything, starting when we were kids. When I was in elementary school, I was very intelligent. (Yeah, I don't know what happened either.) We would take our standardized tests, and I would always score in the 95th or 99th percentile, meaning that I received higher scores than 95 percent to 99 percent of all kids my age.

When I was a server in the restaurant business, we would track who the good servers were by tracking something called PPA (price per average). It was basically how much money, on average, a customer spent with each server. Do not even get me started on how flawed this system is. (Servers who work in the bar generally had people spend more money on drinks and higher PPAs. Servers who had the bigger booths generally had families with children sit in their sections and, of course, have lower PPAs. It was a mess, but I digress.) Anyhow, statistics makes the world go round, so why would individuals not use them to determine their own personal value?

Throughout my high school and college career, I came up with a system I thought worked perfectly—I could do whatever I wanted in school as long as I was respectful to my parents and teachers and was really good and "Christian-like" in church. If you knew me from church, you would have thought I was a saint—I stood up during worship, I raised my hands, I went up during the altar calls, I went to the all the discipleship classes and all the God Encounter events, I was the perfect Christian; until I drove off the property. If you knew me outside of church and at school, the perception was very different indeed. To me, cursing was allowed in the school hallways, but worship songs belonged in the church. Getting drunk was acceptable with high school friends, but my church friends and I would thirst only for communion. Kissing and degrading girls was perfectly fine in the school cafeteria, but women were to be respected and revered within the sanctuary. Harvey Dent did not have anything on me. (That's a Batman reference for those of you who did not get it. Harvey Dent is the Batman villain known as Two-Face. Come on people, get with your pop-culture references.)

Whenever I did something specifically dastardly or something that stretched even beyond my very limited and low standard of morality, I would justify my actions by comparing myself to someone else. That one (and only one) time I cheated on my church girlfriend by kissing a girl at the school, I made myself feel better by noting that what I did was not nearly as bad as the captain of the baseball team who was cheating on two different girls who were best friends (that really came to a head when they fought at our senior prom, but that's not my story to tell)! It was always easy to find somebody worse off than me. Moral ambiguity seemed like a necessity in high school; and in college, alcohol not only blurred vision and speech, but also morality lines.

My life had become a balancing act. I began to subliminally equate good actions and bad actions and tried to give both sides equal values. When I was in college, getting black-out drunk for an entire weekend meant that I would spend the following weekend spending all my time at the church serving. If I ended up having sex with a girl or doing anything sexual, I found that praying for someone and spending some time listening to his or her problems put my conscience at ease. If I cursed out a classmate during the week, you better believe that I would be giving someone a word of encouragement that Sunday. It was the perfect system (or so I thought).

It never made any sense to me how some people could be foolish enough to be themselves all the time. The phrase "be true to yourself" was lost on me. Why "be true to yourself" if it did not give you want you wanted? I preferred the much less well-known "be fake to yourself so that you can have your way and get whatever you want." (I know it's a bit long, which is probably why it is not that popular.) When I was younger, my brothers and sisters classified me as the "good son." When we went to church, I was the one who joined in with praise and worship. I got pretty decent grades in school. I was involved in the really good clubs and organizations, and I actively participated in church events. And if I'm really honest, I reaped the benefits of it. On my sixteenth birthday, I received my first car within a week. When I wanted to go on a school trip or event, my parents were more than willing to pay for it and allow me to go. If I wanted to spend the night at a friend's house, my parents had no problem letting me go.

Many people would look at this and say that this is terrible, that I used manipulation to get my way, and I am promoting it as a tactic that works. This is not true at all. There were terrible consequences to being labeled the good son. The major one being standards. Did you know that some parents do not measure their children on the same level?

My brother could get ten referrals and get grounded one week for each one. (That's ten weeks for all my mathematicians out there.) If I got one referral, I would be grounded for at least four weeks! (That's four times as much as my brother would get punished! Once again, I wanted to clear that up for all the mathematicians.) When I got my car, my parents were overjoyed to explain to me that I would have to get a job in order to pay for gas (the nerve of them). My first job was at the library. Do you know how boring and terrible it is for a sixteen-year-old boy to work at a library? And I actually liked reading. (Oddly enough, this would also be the only job I would ever be fired from.) So for all this newfound freedom I received from being compliant, it added a whole other level and perspective of responsibility I had never even considered.

Not only did it raise the standards of my parents, but it also raised the standards of my friends. Did you know that when you pretend to be nice and considerate to people, they actually expect you to nice and considerate to them *all the time*? The nerve of them. I would spend hours listening to the cares and worries of "friends" that I really just wanted to play video games with, or talk about girls with, or goof around with, or hang out with and "forget" my wallet so they would pay for things. It was exhausting.

Okay, here is another example of Bad Darred that I think perfectly sums up my level of selfishness at this stage in my life. I was hanging out with the "friend" who I used to drink with who invited me to hang out with him and two girls (so my motives for spending time with him: the booze and the girls). Earlier that week, he had broken up with his girlfriend, but for the most part, he acted like it did not affect him. We texted back and forth that day how we were so looking forward to "spending time" with these girls. Yet when I showed up that night, he had already been drinking and was crying hysterically about his ex. I was outraged! How dare he get emotional when I have an opportunity to have sex! (Yeah, I know. You do not have to tell me. It is only by the grace of God that I am the man I am now.) Didn't he know that our friendship was strictly based on the superficial jokes, consumption of alcohol, and degradation of women? I spent the whole night consoling him. (Admittedly, I probably did a terrible job because I was so mad at him.) We never met up with the girls, and I truly felt betrayed by him. Still think that I "got away" with manipulating people?

If the standards of my parents being raised and the standards from my friends did not frustrate me enough, eventually my own standards began to make their presence known. People say that "ignorance is bliss," and that is so true. If you don't know that you are doing something wrong, do you feel bad about what you're doing? Absolutely not! Why would you? You do not think you are doing anything wrong. This was not the case for me, I was painfully aware that what I was doing was wrong. I knew what I was supposed to do as a Christian, I knew what God expected of me, and I just did not want to do it. The problem was that I could not just turn off that fountain of knowledge that I had received from the church. As much as I wanted to, I could not just forget the lessons that I learned, and it affected how I felt doing bad things.

Sex is not nearly as enjoyable when you know that the girl you just slept with is a daughter of God and you did not honor her the way God commands of you. Do not get me wrong, during the act, it felt great, but the guilt and shame afterward was excruciating. A few minutes of physical gratification is not worth days of conviction. Being drunk is a lot less fun when you are constantly reminded that you are grieving the Holy Spirit. Looking down at a person and talking behind their back does not seem as justified when you are reminded that they are God's children.

I was not ignorant of what God was calling me to be. I just refused to give Him everything. I would bargain with God and tell Him when He could have my attention and my actions. I was making demands of Him and telling Him when and how He could have me. And when it seemed like I was being really bad, I just reminded myself I am generally a good person, I could be a whole lot worse than I currently am. I would listen to statistics and use them to make myself feel really good at where I was in life.

One in six young men between the ages eighteen and twenty-five are currently in jail. Only 25 percent of children who spent time in foster care graduated in high school; even less make it to college. One out of every three college students drop out of college after the first year. (Note: these are not accurate statistics. I am just giving examples of information that I would use.) Every time a statistic came up that made me look better, I was quick to grab a hold of it, And by the world's standards, I was doing pretty good. Think about it. When I was a young man, I got a high school diploma and a college degree. I was alive and healthy. I did not get any girl pregnant, and I got pretty good grades. Never mind that I had been arrested and charged with driving under the influence, had about $25,000 in school loan debt, and had what some would view as a drinking problem. Nobody's perfect, right?

Anyone could look at his or her life and say, it could always be worse. But how many people look at it and think it could be better? When we focus on comparing ourselves to societal norms, we are teaching ourselves to settle. Basically, individuals looking at the "stats of life" are saying, "I just need to be better than the rest of these people." When I did that, I did not become the best person I could be. I was just becoming better than the worst people I could find.

The problem with statistic-based living is that they are the only area of an individual's life that is actually impressive. If I were to spend a few pages and give you the statistics of the things I have overcome, I am sure you would be very impressed. Who does not like hearing about someone who beat the odds? That is why people play the lottery. They want to be the one out of millions to overcome the odds. The problem is that a great statistic does not necessarily make for a great story. Look at me for example. Yes, the statistics I have overcome are incredible, but the story has more than a little to be desired.

When people start living their lives based on statistics, they take out the human and personal aspect in life. Statistics says that 50 percent of all marriages end in divorce. That means everyone who gets married has the same chance as a coin toss of their marriage lasting—those are not very good odds. Some would ask, why even get married at all then? The answer is simple—you are not a product of the statistics you live by. You are a product of the environment and relationships you have been a part of.

I remember when I was nominated to be the Pathfinder nominee in debate for my high school. Pathfinder was this incredibly prestigious honor in Florida that recognized students for success in different areas of academics. I cannot accurately convey how big a deal it was to be nominated. Each school only has twelve seniors nominated, and I was one of them. The statistics showed I was pretty important. Yet when I went to the event and heard about all the students who won, I realized how wrong I was to think that.

These teenagers had done incredible things: started nonprofit organizations, gone to national events, competed in international competitions and won, created inventions and patents. These students were beyond amazing. Then there was little old me. I had been on the debate team for a year and placed second in a few competitions. In actuality, I was just really good at talking and arguing with people. I did not have any incredible accomplishments to my name, no major investments to society, just what I wanted and how I wanted it.

That is the difference between living your life based on statistics and living your life based on a story. Statistic-based living says, "It could be worse"; but story-based living says, "It could be better." Colossians 3:23 says that "whatever you do, work at it with all your heart, as working for the Lord, not for human masters." If I offered everything I was doing as a young adult to God, there's no way He would want any of it, regardless of how good it was statistically. That is what I thought for the longest time, but now I realize how wrong it was to think that way.

He does want it—all of my mess, all of my mistakes, everything. God wants it because He can take it and do something beautiful with it. The greatest part of any story in the Bible is when God shows up. The same thing could be said of each and every one of our lives. The greatest part of my life's story is when God showed up. Everything up to now had been a complete mess, but we are finally getting to the part where the statistics did not matter, and God was about to completely change it into an incredible story.

I know it has been quite a challenging story to follow so far but stick with me. We are about to get to the good part.

The Transformation

When I was in the tenth grade, my English teacher introduced our class to something called the Hero's Journey. It is basically the idea that every hero in every story goes through a very similar series of steps that make up their journey. I was actually very intrigued by this concept and always wondered that if someone wrote about my life, what my hero's journey would look like? (Yes, I was arrogant enough to think that people should consider me a hero. I mean, have you been reading this book?)

There are a lot of different steps in the journey and quite a few variations to it as well. So when I wrote this book, I was inclined to put my story into the hero's journey format. I could have broken it up into the many subcategories, but I decided to keep it simple and divided it into what I thought were the three most important steps of the journey These have been represented by the three subtitled areas that are here in this book.

The first one came at the very beginning and is called the Call to Adventure and is the simplest one to understand. It is basically when the individual starts their journey. So naturally, I started my call to adventure at birth—that is why it is at the beginning. This will go on for some time and includes steps such as supernatural aid, finding tools to use, and adding friends and relationships, which I feel were manifested in some form throughout those first four chapters.

After the "Call to Adventure," the next major area is the "Abyss," which is pretty much when all hell breaks loose in the hero's life. If it is in a movie, this is the part where things fall apart, and they show a sad montage of the hero moping around because nothing is how he or she planned them out to be. It is also always the end of the second movie of a trilogy, think *Empire Strikes Back* of the *Star Wars* original trilogy. (Luke was just defeated by Darth Vader. Han Solo is captured by Boba Fett in carbonite, and our heroes are running away from the empire.) Naturally, I decided that the second section of these three parts should be the abyss of my life, and that is a very accurate way to look at it. Even though it may have seemed like everything was okay and great in my life to those who saw me externally, truth be told, internally, I was dying, and it seemed like there was no way out.

Now comes my favorite part—the "Transformation." This is the part where the hero turns everything around and saves the day, the part where the good guys win and overcome evil (*Return of the Jedi* anyone?). That is the section that we are coming to now, and I am so excited to tell you about it. But before I do that, I must clarify something. Yes, this is indeed the hero's journey, but just like I stated before, I am not the hero of this story. As cliché as it sounds, that title belongs to Jesus. Without Him, the story continues with me being in the abyss and never escaping. Unfortunately, that becomes the case with so many people. They try to become the heroes of their own lives and find it an impossible feat.

You are not meant to be hero of your life; Jesus has already saved you. The hero's journey could also be translated to the "He-rose Journey." (I don't care if you think it is corny. When I came up with it, I was ecstatic.) First Corinthians 15:57 states, "But thanks be to God! He gives us the victory through our Lord Jesus Christ." God does not give us victory through our willpower or our own strength, or anything we can do on our own, but only through Jesus Christ.

I know it sounds simple, but it just does not seem to be possible. And believe me, I get it. When life is hard, it can become hard at times to think that Jesus has given us victory. So many people think that transformation is instantaneous, and in some cases, it can be. But if that was true all the time, I could simply tell you the story of how God came to me, and that would be the end (which is what I do plan on telling in the next chapter). But I still have four more chapters, which means there is still more to tell after that happens.

So bear with me because I have made the mistake of thinking that accepting Jesus is all it takes for your life to be put in order. It is as simple as that, but it is not as easy as that. See, I have come to realize that people get those two terms confused. They naturally assume that *simple* and *easy* are synonyms, and they are not. Playing football is simple—get the football from one end of the field to the other end—but it is far from easy. If it was easy, everyone would be in the NFL, making millions of dollars, but there are other challenges that go into the game. There is simplicity in allowing Jesus to take control of your life, but there are other challenges that we face that can make it far from easy.

That is what these last chapters are about, understanding the challenges and how to overcome what prevents us from enjoying the simplicity of loving and accepting Jesus. You have read this far, why would you stop now that you are about to get to the best part?

9

It's Not about What You're Called . . . It's About Who's Calling You

So let's take a moment to recap where we are in this story. I am now in college, living the two-faced life. Inside the church, I am the model of Christianity—raising my hands during worship, volunteering for events, and serving whenever I am needed. Outside of the church, I am the model of living the high life—drinking and partying all the time, going to bars and chasing women, and generally doing whatever I want. The greatest challenge with living two different lives is that you really do not feel like you are a part of either of them.

I felt like the people in the church did not understand me or really have any idea of what fun and excitement was or should be. At the same time, I felt like my friends in the world had morals that were too loose and had no idea how to be better people. Neither group felt like they were truly my friends, and because of that. I was caught in this weird limbo between being around both of them but never really feeling a part of either of them. This made it especially hard to find a girlfriend.

Let me be honest with you, I was never one of those guys who just liked sleeping around and having fun all the time. The overall goal for me was to always find a nice girl to settle down with. (It still is, of course, just not as much time or energy go into it now.) Whenever I would go home with a girl that I was not interested in having a relationship with, I viewed her as more of a consolation prize than an accomplishment. I struggled to find a girl I truly felt understood where I was at, and when you think about it, it is not that hard to see why.

I could not date a girl that I met at the bar because she would not want to come to church with me or understand my commitment there. And I certainly could not date a girl from church because she would not want to have fun with me and join me out for a night of drinking. So I felt like I was stuck, doomed to walk this earth alone, in-between worldly living and godly living. This all changed when I met Suzy.

I met Suzy when I was working. She came in to eat at the restaurant I was working at with her family to celebrate her older brother's birthday. She was gorgeous, and from our short encounter with one another, I could tell she had a great personality. (I know this is the most generic description ever, and one that guys use for almost every girl they think is physically attractive. But Suzy truly was pretty great in my eyes, and I'm sure she still is.) Anyhow, by a strange set of circumstances, I came to find out later that Suzy thought I was pretty cool too. (Take it how you will, I think she just told someone I worked with that she thought I was "super cute.") And I was able to get her contact information and took her out on a date.

It was during this date that I realized that Suzy was a girl I could finally see myself with. She was incredible. She went to the University of Central Florida, just like me. She enjoyed going out drinking, just like me. Yet she was also raised in the church, so had good Christian values, just like me. And she thought I was attractive and fun, just like me. (Just kidding, but I did think she was attractive and fun as well.) For the first time in my three years of college, I finally found a young woman I thought could be girlfriend material, and I was pumped!

The next few weeks were awesome. I felt like I had someone who could relate to me. We would go out with friends to the bar and have a good time, and I could also tell her when I had to go spend time at church and not feel like she was judging me or turned off by that. I also met her parents during that time, who loved me. ("Love" may be a bit strong here, but if there is one area I always thrived in when it comes to dating—it was related to parents category.) Everything was going so smoothly, and life was good. This turn of events made me feel like I was finally justified in living the life I wanted.

At this time, I would like to pause for a moment and address the people who live this type of life. You know who you are, and I do not say any of this with any type of accusation or judgment (How could I? I'm the king of the double life.), but I would like to give you a warning. The double life may last for a while, but it will not last forever.

Matthew 6:24 states, "No one can serve two masters. Either you will hate the one and love the other, or you will be devoted to the one and despise the other. You cannot serve both God and money." (I know the verse ends with the distinction between God and money, but I believe it can apply to other areas as well, such as drinking, worldly living, or sexual immorality against God.)

Here is what I have come to learn about that verse—sometimes your allegiance between those two masters will constantly be shifting. There were times when I would go out drinking and be so angry at the prospect of having to go to church that week. Just the anticipation of going to church would completely ruin my night. Then, the very next week, I would be out again and be so disgusted with myself for how I was acting because I knew better—that I could not stand even being in that bar and once again. It would completely ruin my night. Or I would be in church or serving the church, and I would be bored out of my mind and so irritated by how tedious the work is that I wanted nothing to do with the church and was looking forward to leaving and going to party it up. While, on the flip side, I could go to church and feel so convicted about the junk I had done earlier that week that I felt like I did not even deserve to be in church and was a miserable excuse for a Christian. It is possible to be constantly shifting to which master you love and which one you despise. so much so, in fact, that you end up never truly being able to enjoy either of them.

No matter what situation I was in, or what perspective I took, serving two masters always seemed to make me a miserable wreck, which means that both situations made me feel like the worst person on earth. This is a danger that not a lot of people are aware of, and even less know what to do with it because choosing a side just seems too hard. If I committed wholly to the church, I would miss out on all the fun of drinking and partying, but if I committed wholly to the world, I would feel like a bad person because I knew better than that. So I simply did my best to stay in the middle of the road, and Suzy seemed to be the perfect validation of this tactic. But that would all change very quickly. (I mean, did you really expect anything else?)

This change would come a few weeks of Suzy and I spending time together (once again, not quite dating. Enter generic *pre-dating* term here). On one particular weekend, the church I attended was hosting a youth conference, and they asked me to be the emcee of the event. Basically, I was the hype man. I would introduce speakers, do giveaways, make the kids go crazy, and do silly things. I was really excited about it, so much so that I made sure I did not do any drinking that week (because in my flawed moral perspective that was the best way to prepare myself to serve the church). The conference would last all weekend, from Thursday evening all the way through Sunday night. So since I would be so busy with the conference, I told Suzy I would not be able to hang out with her that week, and she was perfectly okay with that (like I said, she was pretty cool).

So I went to this conference, and honestly, I had a pretty good time. I do not know if you know this about me, but I enjoy attention. And what better way to get attention than being the guy who holds the mic for most of a youth conference? I remember being a kid and hearing all these testimonies about conferences changing lives and completely transforming other teenagers and young adults. If I am completely honest, this did not happen to me one bit. I was not transformed from the speakers. I did not weep and cry out to God during the altar times. To me, this conference was just another event on my Christian half of life. I even considered just how worldly I would be able to be the following week because I was so Christian for an entire weekend. (This was a thought I had *during* the conference!)

Anyhow, nothing major happened during the conference. (At least, not for me. I do not want to diminish God's ability to work in church events, but I do want to emphasize that this change did not occur simply because of an event. But I'm getting off topic.) So I get done with the conference on Sunday evening, and even though I went home each night during the conference, the days were so long I really did not talk to Suzy at all during the conference. Needless to say, I was excited to catch up with her and make plans to spend time with her. So I give her a call Sunday evening and catch her up on the past few days. She then informs me that she was planning on spending the night with some of her girlfriends at home, drinking wine. It is soon after she tells me this that I hear the four dreaded words that are still etched into my brain until this day—"We need to talk."

I know this is probably not news to anyone reading this, but when someone says, "We need to talk," it is never good news. No one ever follows that statement up with something that is really good news, so I was horrified when I heard this over my phone. Yet it was still relatively early in our relationship (I mean we were still "talking" at this point), so I could not overreact. I asked her what she wanted to talk about, and she dived right in by saying this was not working for her. I knew what she meant but felt the need to ask for clarification anyway. We were not working for her. The idea of her and me just no longer gave the excitement it used to give her, and she basically decided that it was time to move on. Once again, due to the brevity of our relationship, I could not overreact. So I didn't, even though I really wanted to.

Once she told me her decision, I was determined not to argue against it, but I did have one question that I needed answered—"Why?" When I first asked this, she was very standoffish, but I persisted in asking her anyway. Relationships are so weird. One moment the person you are with thinks you are the most incredible person in the world and they cannot imagine life without you, and within a short period of time, he or she cannot stand you and is contemplating the most creative ways to kill you to get rid of you. (This is an extreme exaggeration. Please do not contemplate or follow through with killing your significant other.) I have never understood that.

In my brief lifespan, I have only broken off two relationships, and I was devastated each time, pretty much to the same extent as if I had been broken up with. The first time, I was so upset that I did not eat for a week (which, anyone who knows me can attest, is a really big deal for me). The second time I broke up with another young lady, I was so upset it made me physically ill. So for me to see someone break up with me and seemingly have no impact on her is so confusing to me.

Eventually, I managed to coerce a reason out of her, and kudos to her for her complete honesty. She just told me bluntly, "You're just too Christian for me."

Yeah, let that sink in for a moment. The two-faced king of "worldly Christianity" was just accused of being "too Christian." That is at least the way that I took it, an accusation. Immediately, I had to resist the incredible urge to respond with a claims and evidence of just how un-Christian I truly am. I wanted to look back and tell her about on my past trips to the bar, my promiscuous past, my filthy mouth when I was out with college friends, and any other information I felt would put me back on the non-Christian bandwagon. But I didn't because, once again, that would have been an overreaction, and our relationship was too short to really justify that type of action. So I said that was okay and that I wish her all the best, and our conversation was over and that was it.

My initial reaction was shock. It was such an outlandish accusation that I could not fully process it. Is that really how people in the world looked at me? I was too Christian? I knew that could not be true. I knew what it took to be a true Christian, and I hardly met any of the criteria. I very rarely read my Bible, and other than before meals, my prayer life was nonexistent. Sure, I went to church and volunteered quite a bit, but that was more show than anything else. Well, I suppose I put on too good of a show because the people that I allowed to get close to me viewed me as an extreme "Jesus freak."

While at the same time, I thought about my friends in the church and how they would view the other half of my life. They would certainly think I was living it up out in the world and the epitome of secular living.

When I was a kid in high school, my friends would make fun of me that being multiracial made me too much of a race. My white friends would jest about how I was too black to hang out with them because my rap music would be too loud and my pants would be too saggy. My black friends would make fun about how I was too white because my country music was too loud and my skater shoes were too big. So in an effort to be accepted by both groups, it came across that I was rejected by both of them. I realized that night that the same could be said of my secular and Christian lives.

Once the disbelief subsided, anger began to take its place. Who was Suzy to say I was "too Christian"? I most certainly am not "too Christian." If anything, she is "too Christian"! We had been spending time together for a few weeks, and we still had not had sex at all! There were girls I had known only a few hours that were willing to give it up to me! She does not know my life. She does not know how many different church events I did not go to because I was hung over or wanted to go get drunk with my friends. She did not know about how many times I had called and lied to people at the church about not being able to attend an event because I wanted to do something on my own! I had been arrested and charged with a DUI—what kind of Christian does that! Clearly, this girl is foolish to think I was anything close to a Christian just because I went to one church event for a weekend!

Plus, isn't that the type of guy you want to be in a relationship with? Nobody wants to marry someone who is running around, acting a fool, but they want someone who is trying to get his or her act together! Why would I want to be with someone who did not want to be with me because I was trying to improve myself? These thoughts overwhelmed my mind, and I soon realized they were no longer contained in my head as I began to vocalize these concerns.

Soon, my thoughts and words were no longer directed at just Suzy, but at other people who had judged me when I would do things that made me seem "too Christian." I began to get angry with my old roommates who kicked me out of their apartment a year earlier because I was "not as much fun anymore since I started going to church"! How dare they say I am not as much fun anymore, just because there were some days when I just did not feel like drinking! My time in church hardly affected them at all! I never invited them to the church or asked them to change their ways for me!

I yelled about all the coworkers who used to love going out with others and me for drinks after work. Now, hardly anyone I worked with asked if I wanted to go out with them because so often, I would tell them no. Just because I said no most of the time, does not mean I still would not like the option!

My anger shifted once again, but this time, it was directed toward my "Christian friends." This was clearly their fault. If they did not always ask me to hang out with them or expect me to be engaged in the same church activities, I would not have spent so much time away from my college friends. How dare these Christians expect me to be just like them! How dare they think I wanted to spend my nights at their house talking about the Bible, or at restaurants, having "good, clean fun"? Didn't they know how much fun getting drunk was? Instead, they viewed me as a role model who had to set an example for the teenagers in the youth group! The nerve of them!

Again, my focus shifted—this time, to my parents. They had raised me this way, to believe that going to church was the right thing to do. So clearly, this is their fault! They taught me about being a Christian but failed to tell me that not being a Christian was so much fun and that I would miss out on these opportunities if I dedicated my life to the Lord! I had to figure this out on my own. They should have let me make these decisions on my own!

By this point, I am yelling at the top of my lungs and bawling my eyes out. Snot is flowing out of my nose, and I am a complete wreck. (Luckily, my youth pastor was not home to witness this because I am sure he would have thought I was having a break down, and I may have been kicked out right then and there.)

Finally, my anger picks what I view to be the true source of all of my problems—God. I snarl and give God the full extent of my anger. "How could You do this to me? What more do You want from me? Within the past few years, You have taken away my roommates, my coworkers, and my drinking buddies! And for what? What did I gain from spending time with You, God? Why am I so interested in making You happy and being obedient to You when You clearly do not care about me? What has God ever done for me? He does not care about my life; my life is a complete joke! Nobody cares about me because of Him! I can't be happy with my worldly friends because I feel indebted to Him, and I can't be happy with my church friends because I am not committed to Him as they are to Him. He probably does not even care about me, and why would He? What has God ever done for me? Doesn't He even know how bad my life is? Everything in my life is ruined! My identity is a mistake! Everything in my life is a mistake! I was a mistake! Everything about me is a mistake!!!! I'm a mistake!!!!!!!"

At this point, I collapsed in exhaustion. All my energy seemed to be expended by this point, and I could not muster up anything else. In order to fully understand the next part of the story, I have to quickly explain something about my past. You see, when I told God I was a mistake, there was a very specific reason that I believed that. At the beginning of this book, all those chapters ago, I told you that my childhood was consolidated to a large folder of paperwork, and that is true. All I have from my years of foster care is that folder, and in it, I found some very interesting information when my parents let me look through it when I was eighteen years old.

If you recall, the only memoir I have from my biological father is a letter he left with my brother and I when he left us. In case you forgot about the letter, I have included a transcript of it again below:

> To Whom this letter may concern. I, the father, of one Darren King Hayes Jr. and also Darian Michael Hayes. I hereby am leaving them in the custody of one, Shawn _____, two Chester _____, and third Angela Marie _____ until I can care for them. The reason for this is because their mother is neglecting them. She [is] out of the house because of her refusal to come home in the evenings. Of the days she's sleeping often. If she tries to reclaim them she cannot. The socalled

mother Nicole admitted to having problems with drugs. Her actual name is Arlene Lee _____. Records indicate as always running away from problems. If she come[s] back while I, the father, am at work she is not to take them. The authorities should be called to investigate her whereabouts if she returns.

Darren King

If you look very closely, my father states that he is the father of two boys. One is named Darian Michael Hayes (that is my younger brother) and the other is named Darren King Hayes Jr. My name was originally "Darren," and I was named after my biological father. Yet that is not my name now, and it had not been my name since I can remember. I have always been called Darred. I asked my parents about this mysterious name change, and they did not have an answer. When I discovered this in the files, I began to investigate but could find nothing to explain the change. There were no name-change forms or documentation of any kind that justified my new name. Yet for whatever reason, at some point between when I was four or five, my name changed from Darren to Darred.

The only possible evidence I could find was a form that was filled out during that time that I found in the folder where the person filling it out sloppily wrote my name, and the lower case *n* at the end of my name looked a bit like a capital *d*. After that form, it seemed that all other paperwork identified me as Darred.

People ask me all the time where my name comes from because they have never heard the name Darred before (and if your name is indeed Darred, then you, my friend, are awesome). For the longest time, I did not know, so I did not have an answer. Yet to the best of my knowledge, my name is simply a mistake that someone made on a form over twenty years ago. The most identifiable trait of me, my name, was a mistake. When I first found this out, I did not really think too much of it. I liked my name and enjoyed the uniqueness of it. Sure, it was hard sometimes when I meet people for the first time, and they could not get it right immediately. But when they did figure it out, they certainly did not forget it.

Yet in my rage against God on this particular evening, my name was a curse. It was a reminder of just how insignificant I truly was. It was a constant rebuttal against the fact that I mattered. And the fact that God had allowed it to happen showed just how little He cared for me and just how much I did not matter to Him. So I threw it in His face. I told God I was a mistake and that He treated me like a mistake—just like how the rest of the world treated me as a mistake, ever since the day I was born.

So there I was, exhausted and enraged at God for putting me into this place and not doing anything to care for this mistake that was lying before Him. It was in this moment that God spoke to me for the first time ever in my life. Before this, I never understood it when people would say that they heard from God, and honestly, I do not think I can do it justice here by trying to explain it. Did they hear a voice from the sky? Was it booming and terrifying to listen to? Did it sound like Morgan Freeman?

When God spoke to me, it was none of these things. The best way I can explain it is that it was just a thought in my head, but different somehow. My inner voice is very sarcastic and always going, so it sounds very fast. This time though, my thoughts were different. It was slower, softer, more intentional thoughts that were just different. That is not to say that this is the only way God speaks to people. I believe He speaks in a variety of ways, and who are we to limit how God speaks? I have seen God speak through other people. I have had him speak through books (especially through the Bible), and I am a firm believer that God can speak to us any way He wants. This time, He just happened to speak to me this particular way.

When God spoke to me in one of my weakest moments ever, this is what He said, "Darred, you are not a mistake. If you had carried the name of your biological father, you would have carried the legacy attached to that name. Darren would have been a drug addict, a dead-beat dad, and one who does not take responsibilities for his actions, but Darred will be a world-changer, he will be a leader, and he will be my son that I love. So, do not think that I do not care about you because I care about you enough to give you a new name, to give you a new family, and to give you a new life. Do not fight it, just simply let me give you what you need, all you need to do is let go of what is unnecessary."

I like to tell people that you know it is God speaking to you because it always sounds better than what you would say, and this was a million times better than anything I could think of to encourage myself, which is why I am so confident it was God who spoke to me.

After this, all the anger, depression, and loneliness subsided. I cannot explain what happened in that exact moment, but luckily, the Bible can. Philippians 4:7 states, "And the peace of God which transcends all understanding, will guard your hearts and your minds in Christ Jesus." Even though it was in complete anger against God, this was probably one of my first genuine prayers to God in my adult life. And He is such a good heavenly Father that He did not answer my anger with anger, but with love.

I had spent so much of my time in college worrying about what other people thought of me that I was consumed by what they called me. I wanted my old roommates to call me their friend and a party animal. I wanted my coworkers to call me fun and desire to spend time with me. I wanted girls to view me as a guy to be desired and sought-after. Yet at the same time, I wanted my youth pastor to call me a good disciple. I wanted my Christian friends to call me a good Christian and a role model. And I wanted my parents to call me a good son. I was trying to be whatever people called me, regardless of who they were and what they thought about me.

I was never really concerned with God and what He called me. That never really mattered because it never seemed to have any impact on my life, but chasing after other people's opinions had a huge impact on me. And no matter what I did, it was never enough for them. That is when I realized that if you chase after what people call you or think about you, you will never feel satisfied. That is because people are fickle. For the past three years, I taught middle school students, and they are the perfect example of fickly people. I have watched young teenage girls who were best friends in the morning but ready to kill one another by lunchtime. Now, this is an extreme example of this, but the concept is still the same.

As you spend more time with people, your perception of them will change, whether for good or bad. It is just a natural occurrence of life. The great thing is that in some cases, your relationship with some people will become so strong they will still be there for you, regardless of how their perception of you have changed.

Sometimes, it is not even the fact that you are different; it is just people's perceptions that have changed. When I was in school, I was pretty much the exact type of student all throughout the years: I was a socially awkward, intelligent student, who got good grades and was really engaged in class, for better or for worse. In elementary school, I remember being classified as an overachiever because of this. When I moved on to middle school, my dominant classification was nerd. After this, in high school, people primarily viewed me as a leader. And in college, I was predominantly viewed as a role model—same person, same personality, different identities.

So it is not about what people call you—people can call you anything for any reason. The true value comes from who's calling you. You want to know what your close friends think of you more than you care about a stranger's opinion of you. The same can be said of God. In my adolescence, I valued the opinions of everyone else over the opinion of the God who created me.

This is why I felt so out of place, because my identity was grounded in what everyone thought of me, and everyone had a different opinion of who I was and who I should be. Hebrews 13:8 says, "Jesus Christ is the same yesterday and today and forever." This also means that His opinion of you does not change. No matter what, God is going to love you. No matter what you do, Jesus was still willing to die for you. This is what I learned that day, lying on the floor, feeling completely alone and abandoned. It did not matter what anyone else thought or how much they thought I had changed. The only opinion that truly mattered was God's, and through that, He would take care of everything else.

I rededicated my life to the Lord that night, right there on my bedroom floor. I prayed and asked Him to forgive me for everything I had done. I had prayed before when I was a kid, but I had fallen so far away that I wanted to start fresh. From that moment on, I knew God had to be a priority in my life. I knew that what He thought of me was far more valuable than what anyone else thought. Yet this was just the beginning of this journey, the beginning of the transformation.

Too often, too many people make the mistake of thinking that giving their life to God means that life gets easier and, like I have said in a previous chapter, following God makes life simpler, but not easier. There is a big difference. Making this decision came with a fair share of new challenges, but I have not once regretted making that decision. And for those of you who are unsure exactly what God's opinion of you is, allow me to share just a few short verses that do a great job telling you just that.

> How great is the love the Father has lavished on us, that we should be called children of God! (1 John 3:1)
>
> The Lord appeared to us in the past, saying: "I have loved you with an everlasting love; I have drawn you with loving-kindness." (Jer. 31:3)
>
> He who did not spare his own Son, but gave him up for us all—how will He not also, along with Him, graciously give us all things? (Rom. 8:32)
>
> Call to me and I will answer you and tell you great and unsearchable things you do not know. (Jer. 33:3)
>
> He will wipe every tear from their eyes. There will be no more death or mourning or crying or pain, for the old order of things has passed away. (Rev. 21:4)

I know it does not always feels like it but believe me when I say that God loves you and He will never stop loving you no matter what. He calls you His love, and that is more important than anything else anyone could ever dream of calling you. It's not about what you're called; it's about who's calling you.

10

——◦◦◦~◦◦~◦◦——

Making Mistakes Doesn't
Make You a Mistake

I f this were a movie, this chapter would be the credits, especially
in a romantic movie. When I look back at it, my relationship
with God truly is a romantic movie (probably more along the
lines of a romantic comedy because of my involvement in it). My life
is a romantic movie that shows just how much God loves me, but
it is also so much more than that. Every romance ends up with the
guy and girl getting together after all the trials and riding off into the
sunset, but what about after that?

I have heard it said that the biggest trouble that married couples
will face would occur in the first few years of their marriage. I am not
going to lie; I did not take any time to find out if this is a true fact.
But just based on my personal experience with friends who are newly
married couples, there seems to be a bit of truth to that statement.
Why is this the case? That's easy—it is because people pursue movie
relationships.

Movies have taught us that all you need to worry about the
pursuit and the goal of getting together—after that, it is all smooth
sailing. Any person who has been married for any amount of time
will tell you that idea is just plain foolish. I have had almost every
married man I know tell me that the biggest challenge does not come
with getting a woman to walk down the aisle toward you but build-

ing a life together with your wife (which really scares me because it seems like it is impossible for me to get a woman down to aisle, but that is not important).

Unfortunately, too many people take this same mentality into their relationship with God: If I could just get down the aisle and to the altar to God, then He will take care of all my problems and life will be perfect. I hate to be the bearer of bad news, but that is just not true. I once heard Joyce Meyers (Does not matter if you know who she is. But if you are curious and do not know her, I highly encourage you to look her up.) say something about people's perception of their relationship with God that I love so much! She said, "Too often people spend ten years serving the world and the devil, and expect God to clean it up in ten minutes." Sadly, I was one of these people.

Now that I had dedicated my life to the Lord, I was ready for him to just come and fix all my problems. Now that the blood of Jesus cleansed me, I just knew I was also cleansed from my desire to party, my desire to have sex, and my need to be accepted by people around me. My romance with God was complete, and I was ready to ride off into the sunset and the rest of my life would be the perfect Christian walk. In all honesty, the exact opposite happened.

We have all heard the word *temptation* and the Bible talks about a lot about it. Yet temptation is not just for the people who do not know Jesus, but also for even the most dedicated Christians. When I had my "come to Jesus" moment, temptation struck harder than ever before. No one wanted to hang out with me or invite me to go partying with him or her before I fell on my bedroom floor and cried out to God. After that happened? The texts and invitations came flooding in! In those first few weeks, I turned down more invitations to go out and get drunk than I received in my first three and a half years of college. People even offered to pay my way, to buy my drinks—it seemed like everyone I ever drank with before missed me and wanted to be drinking buddies again! (#thestrugglewasreal.)

Before this time, I could not buy a girlfriend (not that I would ever do that, but you get my point), but now, girls were—okay, so they were not exactly throwing themselves at me, but there were a couple of them who were interested in me now. And a couple is a whole lot more than zero. There would be one instance a few months down the road where I went out with some coworkers (to a little burger place, just to get some food, no drinking), and one of the most drop-dead gorgeous girls there pretty much wanted to "get with me." Right there . . . in her car . . . in the parking lot. I know what some of you guys are thinking—"What an idiot!" I would be lying if I did not think the same thing as I told her good night and got out of her car and walked by to my own (ran back would be more appropriate).

The old life that I had walked away from was a jealous ex, and it was doing everything it could to get me back. I have come to realize that this is the way the enemy (devil, Satan, Lucifer—you know who I'm talking about) gets people to fall back into that lifestyle. The devil will do whatever it takes to get you away from God. So before this, the devil fed me depression, anger, and loneliness, and he gave me just enough of the world that I still clung to the idea of finding happiness on my own.

Yet I reached that point where it felt like nothing mattered and turned to God. The moment that this happened, the devil pulled out all the stops, and nothing was going to keep him from winning me back. He threw the girls at me, the drinks, the parties, and the friends, and tried to show that happiness could be found in this immoral lifestyle.

In this past, this had worked. During my high school years, I knew that having sex and getting drunk was wrong, but I was okay with being wrong if it felt good and made me feel loved and appreciated. So what was the difference between this time and every other time before it? In the past, I had the head knowledge of Jesus, but not the heart belief.

Allow me to go "boring mode" for just a moment because I believe this is important for Christians to understand. So many people gain an understanding of who God is, and they make a decision to give their life to Him. They ask for forgiveness. They say they are going to change and that lasts for about three weeks.

The problem is that they believe in their mind but not in their heart. What do I mean by that? You have to *love* God—I mean, really, truly *love* Him in order to really get it. If not, it feels like an obligation instead of a privilege. With that being said, the goal of this chapter is my very feeble attempt to explain what that love looks like. Don't get me wrong, you are about to read about a *lot* more of the mistakes I made after committing to God. (Yeah, they still happened.) The only difference is that this time, I truly loved God, and I felt conviction, not condemnation. Conviction is that feeling that says to you, "I can't believe I messed up, I have got to do better." Condemnation is the feeling that says, "I can't believe I messed up, I'll never be good enough. I should just give up." The fact remains is that none of us are good enough, but thankfully, God gave us a way where we can make it. But you already know about that, so let's move on to the new stuff.

Let us start with the most basic of these temptations and struggles that I now faced—the external ones. These were the ones I had no control over. These were the distractions that simply came to me, and I had to deal with them as they came. Just because I was a different person, does not mean that the world became a different world. Not only that, being different does not mean anyone in the world even see me any differently. To many of my coworkers, I was still the guy who provided comic relief on an almost daily basis, who was more than willing to participate in the crude humor, making fun of guests, going out drinking and partying, and being extra generous if I got really drunk. (I honestly think this is the primary reason many of them enjoyed having me around.) Why would they think any differently?

I still looked like the same person. I talked like the same person. And I acted like the same person. The only difference they really noticed was my change in desire. I no longer wanted to go party. I no longer wanted to be a part of the crude humor. And I did not enjoy making fun of people and drinking anymore. Basically, according to my coworkers, I became boring.

This is the first misconception I would like to address. Being a Christian is not boring. I would argue that if you're a Christian and bored by it, you're not doing it right. It should be exciting—never knowing what God is going to ask of you today, not knowing whose life you could have the opportunity to impact, and spending time with God and other Christians who love Him. It's a great life, if you do it right! I will admit that it did take some time for me to get adjusted to being committed to God. In the past, when I got bored of the Christians I hung out with, I would simply go spend time with my party animal friends.

Admittedly, not being able to find a suitable alternative to drinking did cause me to fall off the wagon a few times. That's right, even after making up my mind and being completely sold out to God, I ended up getting drunk again! I'm sorry if this is not your story; perhaps when God came into your life, you dropped every bad habit and never looked back. If that is the case with you, that is absolutely awesome, but it just was not the way it went down in my life. I struggled with the idea of not partying anymore because choosing between going to Denny's after a youth service or going to a bar with half-priced drinks just did not seem like a difficult or a remotely close choice. My urge and desire was almost always to go get drunk.

There are some of you right now who wholeheartedly agree with the previous statement made. Drinking is good! Sex is good! Making fun of people is good! The problem with that mentality is that good is the enemy of great. I could argue before my transformation that I had a good life. Sure, I had made some mistakes along the way, but who didn't? But now, after having this incredible encounter with God, I saw what it was like to have a great life. And good just did not seem good enough for me anymore.

Now, I know many of you are wondering what my stance is on drinking since I have mentioned it so many times by now. Very simply, I *nothing* drinking. Yeah, you read that right. I don't like drinking, but I also don't hate drinking. I nothing it. In the past, I would drink to relate better to the people around me, to lose my fears and inhibitions, to feel connected to those around me. I no longer need to drink for those reasons; God has helped me relate to those around me. The strength of the Holy Spirit has helped me overcome fears and inhibitions. And being a part of a church community has allowed me to feel connected to others.

So if you drink, don't look at me to be the one to condemn you. Personally, I don't believe that it adds anything of value to my life or my ministry, so I don't need it. For those of you think that it makes me less relatable to people who do drink, I would say that you're completely wrong. My last year of college allowed me to become one of the most sought-out brothers to go out to bars with in my fraternity (because everyone knew I could be the designated driver). Just earlier this year, one of my friends was celebrating a promotion and wanted me to join him and his friends. We went out to a bar, and I sat down with them sipping on water. We talked, we laughed, and I drove everyone home.

Eventually, I found out that going to Denny's after youth group could be fun; I just had to create an atmosphere that I enjoyed. And I know what some of you are thinking—you would never trade a night of drinking for a night of pancakes. That's fine; I would never trade a morning of waking up with a stomach full of pancakes with a morning that is completely ruined by a hangover. But please do not get too upset with me here; I am not here to preach or condemn anyone with this book. I'm just trying to tell you what I have done.

Another reason that drinking does not hold any major influence over me now is that it was a symptom of another major issue I was dealing with—disconnect and intimacy. Like I said, I drank to feel connected to people, and even though I had accepted God, I still struggled with loneliness. I knew God was with me wherever I went, but for some reason, there were so many times that I did not feel Him with me. So while I struggled somewhat with drinking, I really struggled when it came to the opposite sex.

When I first had my major conversion, I was thoroughly convinced that I was finally ready for God to send me my wife. Ha-ha-ha-ha-ha-ha-ha-ha-ha-ha-ha-ha-ha-ha-ha-ha!!!! Yeah, I was very wrong about that. Soon after I rededicated my life, this girl came into my life out of nowhere, and she came after me with all she had. The most ironic part was that I met her in church. I was leading a small group of young adults, and this girl came in. She was cute and seemed sweet. Within the first night of meeting her, I had already had her phone number and was making plans to meet with her that week.

(Short disclaimer: Not everyone who goes to church is a Christian. Not even everyone who says they are a Christian is a Christian. Yet that does not mean they belong in the church.)

In fact, if we truly follow Jesus's example, they are the ones who truly belong in the church. My mistake was I knew this young lady was not a Christian, but simply her attendance in church qualified her enough to pique my interest. We ended up hanging up a few days after meeting at her house (just the two of us). I don't care if you are Jesus's little brother or sister—if you are not married, never be alone with someone of the opposite sex in a private place. You are just begging for trouble. Long story short, we "fooled around" (not sex, but everything else that you could possibly do in that setting). The crazy thing was is that this was not like any of the other times. I was beyond disappointed and ashamed of myself.

Admittedly, I did not handle that situation very well. (I literally avoided her like a plague for the next month until she eventually left the church, but not before she made quite the scene by cursing me out in the church parking lot for "using and abusing her.")

This was different from my high school avoidance maneuvers I used to get girls to break up with me. This time around, I was so ashamed and desperate to follow God that I ran from temptation. Now, in some cases, this is completely necessary, but she deserved some sort of explanation. But I was so terrified that it would happen again, I could not bring myself to initiate contact with her.

There would be one other time that a similar situation happened, which I mentioned earlier in this chapter, and I did a much better time the second time around. I was still serving in the restaurant business, and we had just hired a beautiful new hostess named Molly. I should also state that I was dating a nice Christian girl at the time, but this was still somewhat early in our relationship. Anyhow, even after rededicating my life to the Lord, I still struggled with flirting. If anything, flirting came even more naturally to me because I knew who I was and was sure that I would be able to repel any advances. (Yes, being born again apparently did not make me any less of an idiot. It took a while for God's wisdom to really take hold of me.) So I flirted with this girl, and she responded. And I just need to stress again that she was really, *really* pretty. So we hung out with a group of coworkers one night (eating at a late-night burger place), and afterward, somehow I ended up alone with Molly, in her car.

Oh wow, how history repeats itself. This time, I would not have just been hurting God, but also hurting my girlfriend. I think God knew what He was doing in aligning my relationships and the timing of it because even though I did not end up marrying my girlfriend at the time, I truly don't know if I would have been able to resist Molly's advances that night if I was not dating my girlfriend at the time. I would like to be confident and tell you that I would have trusted in God and He would have made a way for me to escape, but I think having a girlfriend at the time was God's infinite wisdom at work. I got out of that car without so much as a hug exchanged and sprinted straight to my car and drove home.

Later on, I would tell Molly I could not do anything with her because I had a girlfriend. (I was such a coward. I could not even mention my dedication to God.) The crazy thing was that when I told Molly this, she pursued me even harder! Saying that she was so attracted to the fact that I was such an honest, nice, and upstanding man! I'll be honest, I kind of get that thought process, but then I don't. (If you're a young lady and would like to help me, I would be more than willing to meet with you and discuss it . . . In a public place, with one hundred of our closest friends.)

So basically, I have already explained to you about my awesome encounter with God and how He completely transformed my life so I would never be the same again. And now, I'm telling you about bad stuff I did *after* God changed my life. I know that I am unique and special, but I truly believe I cannot be the only one who has had a true encounter with God and still struggled with areas that they believed God had delivered them from. Romans 12:2 states, "Do not conform to the pattern of this world, but be transformed by the renewing of your mind. Then you will be able to test and approve what God's will is—His good, pleasing and perfect will." Paul is writing this letter to the Christians of the Church of Rome.

Why would Paul write this if it is already expected that the moment someone becomes a Christian, they no longer struggle to be like the world? That does not make any sense; it must mean that Paul knew Christians would still struggle with things in the world. The same way that I struggled with drinking and girls after my conversion is the same way that people struggle with areas in their life before God came into it. Does that mean that it is okay to just continue with these actions because we will never get past them? Absolutely not! I do not drink at all anymore, and even though you might not believe it, there have been more than a few girls who have given me their attention whom I have been able to turn down or avoid. But it is a process, and one that needs to be described and taken seriously.

Now, I should explain that becoming and learning how to be a better follower of Christ is twofold because it is not enough to just stop doing bad stuff. The most frustrating thing that you can do to a child is to tell them to stop doing something without offering some sort of alternative.

This is why if you tell a toddler to stop throwing his or her toys, they will stare at you in confusion. His or her brain is trying to compute what the use of toys is if not to be thrown. This is why you have to show them how to play with toys appropriately—even when you do that, it is going to take a child some time to figure out how to play with a toy the way that it was intended. The same could be said of new Christians, and I know this because I was there. I was not just bad at stopping wrong actions; I was also really bad about doing the right actions.

I will say that I had a bit of an advantage that many people who initially decided to follow Jesus do not have, and that was previous training. I had been raised in church for quite some time, so I knew that right things to do. Yet even with that being said, that means absolutely nothing. I am big believer (and have said numerous times) that knowing the right thing is not hard, but *doing* the right thing is the challenge.

There are times where that seems downright impossible. And immediately after my commitment to God, it was impossible. I knew all the rules and all the things I should have been doing and could have given all the right answers, all the right Bible verses, and all the right steps to take, but I just could not seem to just do it. (Nike must know something with that motto.)

I knew that I was supposed to read my Bible. I knew that I was supposed to pray every day. I knew that I was supposed to tell my friends about Jesus. I knew that I was supposed to worship and go to church all the time, and fast, and memorize the Scripture, and so on. (You get the point!) As much as I knew these things, even though I loved God (and believe me, I truly loved God), I just did not want to do these things. They were hard and, most of the time, boring.

Fellow Christians reading this are outraged at this point. Devout believers have put down this book and have begun to pray and declare heresy at this honest statement from someone who claims to "love God." They may be outraged, but it is the truth. I think if more Christians were honest, they would be able to admit that when they started their journey with God, they found themselves, more times than not, in over their head or just plain bored. I remember days when I could not pray for more than five minutes without wanting to take a nap. I know there was times when I would rather read the nutrition facts on a cereal box than read my Bible. (Sometimes, I actually did that.) Yet I am not ashamed to admit that because I have grown past it, and I can honestly say that I do not feel that way anymore.

Think about when you first started a new sport or new hobby (painting, drawing, writing, etc.). I am sure we could all admit that we were terrible at it. When I first started running track, I thought running was the dumbest thing ever! "Then why did you run track, Darred?" you may ask. Because I wanted to be faster, a winner, and more athletic! Basically, I wanted to be better, and I eventually developed a love for track.

Athletes can tell you that when they started their sport, they may have done it for love of the game, but they did not like the disciplines that came with improving their skills. Learning the basics of drawing and painting would frustrate any up-and-coming artist, but they persevere because they love the art itself. I could not stand the disciplines of being a Christian, but I love Jesus Christ so much I wanted to grow and learn more about Him.

Eventually, my mentality would shift, but that took some time. After a while of getting constantly bored with reading the Bible, I just kept reading the books in the Bible that I enjoyed—Judges, 1 Samuel, and 2 Samuel. I loved these books because they told stories of judges completely destroying other kingdoms, along with the struggles of various kings of Israel and the wars Israel faced were a backdrop to these incredible men overcoming personal and national adversity (primarily David though, I love me some David). At first, five minutes was too much to bear in prayer time, eventually that time shifted to ten minutes, then fifteen minutes, and so on. Now, I could easily spend one or two hours talking to God and just going over every part of my life with Him. This did not happen overnight. It has taken me years to get to this place. There are still some days where I forget to spend time with God in prayer or taking time to read the Bible, or just do not feel like worshipping during church. Yet I am a whole lot better now than I was years ago. Like anything worth having, a relationship with God takes work.

I have a theory, and I do not have any Scripture to support it (even though I am sure that if I worked really hard, I could find some way to pick a random Bible verse to help me explain it). That theory is this—Jesus showed us exactly what it looks like, and even how long it might take, to become just like Him. So follow me here for a minute, I am going to give you some information and make some connections that all have a purpose. I promise.

Jesus did not start being the Jesus we know and read about in the Bible until He was thirty to thirty-three years old. Yes, as a child, He was obedient and never sinned and was probably the perfect child (and all the parents are asking, "How can I get one of those?"), but He did not do any miracles until He was an adult, which is when He started His ministry. So this tells me, that it took Jesus (the perfect example of God, mind you) more than thirty years to get to a place where He was ready to use His perfection to help people. This means it should take every Christian at least thirty years to be like Jesus. Now all the people who are over thirty are saying, "Of course, that makes sense"—but wait, there's more!

Before I could start to be like Jesus, I had to deal with all the junk in my life that pushed me away from God because Jesus never had to deal with all that. Jesus did not have to deal with drinking problems, intimacy problems, and just an overall sinful nature because He was born without sin.

So in my life, I had to deal with twenty-two years of sin in my life, and let us just say that it takes the same amount of time to overcome something as it took me to struggle with it. So since I struggled for twenty-two years, it takes me twenty-two years to deal with all that stuff. That means that I am not ready to proclaim to be completely like Christ until I am at least forty-four! But that is just the start! Once I deal with all the things wrong in my life that means that I am only where Jesus started when He was born! Even though Jesus did not have to deal with all those things, He still spent thirty-plus years preparing, which means once I have dealt with all my junk, I now have at least thirty years to get where Jesus was when He started His ministry. And that's if I live my life perfectly from that moment on! And I just told you about all the times I messed up even after completely submitting to God, which means I still have to deal with things after that point. So I can conservatively say that if you take my twenty-two years of junk and the twenty-two years that it takes to get past that junk and then thirty years of preparation like Jesus, I will be just like Him at the awesome and vibrant age of seventy-four! Yay?

Now, once again, I do not know if this is necessarily true, and I have no way of proving it, but the evidence does support it. I know more than a few people who started serving the Lord at a younger age than me, and they just seem to be closer to God than I am. This is because they have less junk to deal with and more time to spend becoming like Jesus. At the same time, I have also spent time with people who started following Jesus later in life, and for a shorter time than I have and they too seem to be closer to Jesus than I am. For those individuals, I have no answer to explain that. I can only assume they are the exception to the rule. Or my theory is completely wrong (which could be possible, but it makes sense, doesn't it?).

The point of that whole (and possibly false) illustration is to say that no one becomes like Jesus in a day. Or a week. Or a month.

Or even a year. It takes time, so do not be discouraged like I was when you find it hard to read your Bible—or it is difficult to pray or worship. Do not worry. You are not broken. You are just growing. It will come with time—the same way that a basketball player improves his or her jump shot, or a quarterback perfects his passes, or a tennis player increases the strength of her backswing. I can honestly say that with a continued pursuit of Christ comes a continued growth of love and appreciation for time in prayer and His Word (a.k.a. the Bible—I do not make assumptions that everyone understands any term).

My desire as a Christian has shifted from when I was first following God to where I am at now. I used to pray that God would make me the best Christian ever, to make me so much like Jesus that people got Him, and I was confused, and I believe that is God's desire for my life. But He wants me to work for it. He wants it to take the time and discipline so that I truly appreciate and treasure what He has done for me. So I changed my request. No longer do I ask to be the best Christian ever. I ask to be the best Christian I can possibly be each day. I ask for God to make me more like Jesus today than I was yesterday. I believe this change in requests and change in mentality is a result of maturity and growth in Jesus.

The First Epistle to the Corinthians 13:11 says, "When I was a child, I talked like a child, I thought like a child, I reasoned like a child. When I became a man, I put the ways of childhood behind me." This is exactly what I believe happens to us as we dedicate our lives to the Lord. When we first start, so many Christians struggle with the childlike things they had done before they accepted Jesus, just as a child would. We go back to the bad lifestyle choices. We make the same mistakes, but something is different this time. We now know that those things are wrong, but we do not know what to do instead. So we struggle like a child to grasp the correct way to live life, the correct way to grow and mature, and we battle against the old sinful nature.

Unfortunately, that is as far as some Christians get. They decide following Jesus is too hard. The reward does not seem great enough, and the work just does not seem to be making a difference. Yet for those who endure and move past that feeling of failure and take the time to learn the right way to live, they begin to truly enjoy life as time goes on.

I tell people all the time that when I first truly committed myself to the Lord, my life sucked. My old friends did not like me and wanted nothing to do with me, and many of my Christian friends did not believe me. Life was hard, and I spent more time alone than I ever had before. But it was in those alone times that God showed me He was right there with me, pushing me closer to Him. As difficult as that time was, I would not trade it for the world because I love my life now (and even still, it is far from perfect). I know plenty of athletes who tell me how much they hate practicing, but ask an athlete after they win a big game if they would get rid of that practice time and I am sure none of them would trade it for anything. God knows that, so He makes seeking Him even more rewarding than things that we seek in the world.

In John 10:10, Jesus says, "The thief comes only to steal and kill and destroy; I have come that they may have life and have it to the full." Jesus promises us a full life, not an easy life. A full life is not without its ups and downs, but the ups are so high and glorious, and the downs do not seem as bad as they used to because we do not have to face them alone.

11

———◦○C⌒⊃○◦———

Doing the Right Thing
Doesn't Always Feel Right

H ave you ever felt like you were being punished for doing the right thing? You made a decision to help someone, to go out of your way to serve someone else, you made a move to do something to improve yourself, and you get completely criticized for it. That has to be one of the worst feelings on earth. It was also exactly how I felt when I rededicated my life to God at the age of twenty-two. I expected support from friends and roommates, and I think the earliest response they gave me was ridicule. If I am not mistaken, one of my roommates laughed for about five minutes straight and finally asked, "You're not really going to try that Jesus thing AGAIN, are you?" You see, I am not sure if I had mentioned it before, but my encounter with God on my bedroom floor was about my one hundredth attempt to follow God.

The difference this time compared to all the others? This time, I knew who God was. I wanted to love Him because I finally understood how much He loved me. Before this point, I knew what was right and wanted to do what was right, but my only reason for doing that was I did not want to go to hell. I did not want to be seen as a bad person. I believe that everything we do in life is either motivated by fear or love. (Think about it—people eat healthy because they *fear* an unhealthy body. Other people eat whatever they want because

152

they *love* food.) My previous attempts to follow God were motivated by fear, instead of being motivated by a true love of God.

With that being said, I believe that my job as a Christian is not to convince people that loving Jesus is the best way to live, but it is to show that Jesus loves us so much that how he tells us to live truly is the best for our lives. I wish I understood that at a younger age because it would have prevented me from going through so much of the pain I have written about in this book. I truly believe and know that God does want the best for me, and all the things He directs me to do are the right things for my life. Unfortunately, when I made that decision, a lot of my friends disagreed with me and had no problem making their opinions known.

This chapter is a hard one to write because the message I am trying to convey does not necessarily come across as super inspirational but more of a warning. Since committing myself to God, I have tried my best to do the right thing at all times (and failed miserably so many times), but there have been quite a few times that it just did not feel like what I was doing was right.

Take for example my relationships after I rededicated my life to God. You read how bad I was at dating and being in a relationship and how I pretty much used girls, yet when I decided to follow God, I recognized what I was doing wrong and wanted to protect young ladies as the beautiful daughters of God they are. Now, I must confess that I was not completely successful at doing protecting young ladies like I intended, but I did try much harder than I did before Christ.

Soon after making this decision, I met a young lady that started attending a young adults' group that had just started at our church. She was cute and seemed nice and was instantly interested in me. Looking back on it, I can honestly say I was not at a place that I should have been pursuing any type of relationship with any type of girl, but I was young and stupid. And through a series of unknown events, we ended up exchanging phone numbers, and I ended up at her house less than a week later—*alone*. I would like to tell you that I immediately saw the error of my ways and ran out of that house as fast as I could, but that's simply not the truth. I ended up "fooling around" with that girl and left that night feeling like the worst person ever!

I could not believe that I let myself be drawn back into that situation again! I knew what it was like to love and encounter God, and my love for Him still did not give me the strength to endure that situation! Duh!

I was an idiot, and I would like to make a very bold declaration right now: If you are a man, it is next to impossible for you to be alone with a woman where there is mutual attraction and not have some sort of physical contact. I had basically served myself up on a platter to fall into a trap! Don't do that!

I digress . . . I already spent a chapter talking about my fallacies and shortcomings when it comes to purity and sexuality. This is about attempting to do the right thing, and at first, I failed miserably. I was so ashamed that I messed up that I completely avoided the girl for about three weeks. She would see me at church, and I would run the other way. (You can imagine how great that made her feel—this guy "fools around" with her and basically shuns her.) That's not the part where I did the right thing. Eventually, I realized I needed to address this, so I did. One night, I asked her to meet up (in a very public restaurant) and told her why I had been avoiding her.

Basically, I just said to her that what we did was not right, and I should not have violated or taken advantage of her. I apologized and told her I was in the wrong, and I thought it best for us not to have contact with one another. She then proceeded to curse me out for what seemed like an eternity! She made a variety of exclamations that I was a coward, that I took advantage of her, that this was all a lie just to "hit it and quit it," and a slew of other insults that would not be appropriate for this book, even with the initial disclaimer of transparency. It caused quite the scene in that little diner, but I did what I believed was right. I owned up to my shortcomings and apologized for what I did wrong, and I was rewarded with verbal abuse.

This trend would continue later on when I was in my first Christian-dating relationship. She was a sweet girl that I met at the church, and we started doing everything right. For the most part, we avoided being alone with each other. We both served faithfully in the church, and we set a good example for the students because we were both youth leaders at the time. Eventually, she started to get really frustrated about being called in to do work for the church all the time, which I loved. This caused a bit of division between the both of us, and as time went on, it put more and more of a strain on our relationship.

Now, there is something I must confess about my relationships in high school—I had never really broken up with a girl in high school. (I know that is not a shocker because you already read about the many times I had been dumped.) But the reason was because when I was ready to be out of a relationship, I simply distanced myself from the girl until she broke up with me. To me, this was the easiest way to dissolve the relationship because, in the end, I would be okay because I wanted the relationship to end, and the girl would feel empowered because she initiated the break up. (It also did not hurt that I got some sympathy from other girls who heard I had been dumped.)

While this did not fully protect me from emotional pain, it did help dull some relationships and was a manipulation tactic I got pretty good at using. So when this young lady and I started to drift apart, I was tempted to use this same tactic to get her to break up with me. I knew that after three weeks of me ignoring her, she would be fed up and end it, and I could walk away, guilt- (and girlfriend) free.

Yet I knew it was wrong. I knew she deserved a proper explanation (in person, not via text or letter!), and I had to give it to her. I would go to her house one night, and we would talk for over two hours. She cried and was devastated, and it destroyed me. I felt like the absolute worst person in the world, knowing that I had hurt her so much. In the past, it did not affect me because I never had to deal with the fall out of a breakup. I was easily viewed as the victim and received pity and praise for enduring a relationship with someone who had carelessly cast me aside.

Now, I was the bad guy. No one praised me for breaking off what was a relationship with no future. I knew at this time that I was called to a life of ministry, and it was clear that full-time ministry was not a part of her future. No one really even consoled me because I was the one who had made the decision, so I would have to deal with it on my own. She received plenty of help and support, and I felt completely alone. I do believe she needed that support, but so did I. I did what was right and still felt like I was the one in the wrong. How could this even be possible?

I would ask myself that same question with my next relationship. This new young lady and I would date for a while, and even though we both wanted to serve the Lord, we both struggled with sexual desires for one another. I wanted so much to please God, but we got so close to one another (we had an "on-again, off-again" relationship for over two years) that sexual desires were so strong. I can remember numerous times that we would be in the heat of the moment, and I would try to stop and tell her this was wrong and that we shouldn't be doing that. And she would get so angry with me, spouting how dare I get her aroused and then just stop! If I wanted to stop, I should have done so before she got all "hot and bothered!"

Of course, it was difficult to stop in the moment, and there were a few times where we messed up and ended up having sex. (We had no accountability to anyone really and way too much freedom in our relationship.) When that would happen, I would tell her we need to go talk to someone about it and get some help, and she would get angry all over again and said she did not want anyone in our business and knowing intimate details about us.

Looking back on it now, it is clear to see this was not a positive or healthy Christ-like relationship at all. But when you are in it, you believe that your love for the person is greater than the challenges that you face. I was trying to do the right things—get out of the situations that caused us to stumble, confess my sins to other brothers in Christ who could help me get stronger. But every time her response was negative toward that. These were the right things, but I was being told that they were wrong. These are hard lives to live because things that God view as right are viewed as wrong by the world. Even sometimes, when you do what is right, and everyone views it as right, it still feels wrong.

The toughest challenge I faced in doing the right thing occurred a couple of years ago. Once again, it had to do with a girl (go figure, right?). At this point, I thought I had finally found the woman I would be spending the rest of my life with, and I absolutely could not wait to get that started. She was great; she loved the Lord and was attracted to me. (What more could a guy need, really?) We would have conversations until two or three in the morning. (Who needs sleep when you're completely infatuated?) Everything was perfect, and the rest of my life was coming together as well. I was preparing to start studying for my doctorate degree and looking for a new profession. (I was a teacher at the time and ready to move on to the next thing.) It seemed like God was putting everything into place—the perfect woman, the perfect pursuit of growth, and the perfect job. And that all changed one night in January.

The young lady I was seeing was a few hours away from me while we were "getting to know each other" (my appropriate alternative to the term *talking*), which was not a problem because I was getting ready to move down to the area where she was. And I already had a few job opportunities lined up. Then, one day, everything just changed. No longer were we talking until the early morning hours. We would spend a few minutes on the phone, and she would exclaim she was tired and needed to go to bed. The past two months seemed like a distant dream. (I know what you're thinking, "Darred, you felt this way about a girl after only two months? Are you crazy?" Give me a break. What can I say? I'm a romantic.)

Anyhow, her distant behavior continued on for a week, so I finally decided to make an unscheduled trip to go see her the following weekend. I thought that her seeing me would remind her how she initially felt about me. Long story short, it didn't. She was still distant. So finally, that Saturday night, I decided to confront the issue. I pretty much asked her point blank what was wrong, and she basically said that things were different, and she could not explain why. There were a ridiculous amount of tears. (I think she may have shed one or two as well.) And she kept saying that she was worried about making a mistake by missing out on a great guy like me. (Don't worry, my ego gets deflated very quickly.)

I decided to do the "right thing." I told her that God was not the Author of fear, so if she was afraid that was not from God. I told her that the best thing she could do was to let me go and let God do what He wanted. This young woman that I wanted to spend the rest of my life with was on the edge of our relationship, and I gave her the push to completely leave it behind. I did it because it was the right thing to do, and I knew it was the right thing to do. Yet immediately following that decision, it felt like the worst thing to ever happen to me. For whatever reason, I could not deal with it. I could not shake that loss, even though I was the one who initiated it. Soon after that conversation, the job opportunities down in that area vanished and the idea of getting a doctorate no longer seemed like a great opportunity, but an unbearable burden.

For the next four months, I was in the deepest depression of my entire life. I would wake up in the morning and immediately start crying. I would go to teach and barely make it through class periods, writing instructions on the board, struggling to hold back tears. I was a hollow shell of the man I used to be, and it seemed like no one was there for me.

The only reprieve I got was during free periods and at the end of the school day, where I would turn off all the lights and cry out to God. I would cry out to Him to take the pain away. I would beg Him to not allow me to feel anything anymore. I can even remember telling Him that if this was the way the rest of my life is going to be then I did not want to live any more.

Nothing changed for four months. Now I realize that in the grand scheme of life that four months is not really a big deal when talking about an entire lifetime, but when you're in that depth of depression for over one hundred days, you become truly inconsolable. Sometime between the second and third month, I was thoroughly convinced God spoke to me and told me that if I was patient, that the young lady would actually come back to me, but it still did not provide any real consolation. How could a hopeful future compare to the present hell I was enduring? Romans 8:18 states, "I consider that our present sufferings are not worth comparing with the glory that will be revealed in us." I read that verse every day for four months, and it did little to nothing to alleviate the pain and suffering I was enduring during that time.

It is so easy to offer that verse to those in the midst of trials and hope that it would allow them a semblance of hope. I did not feel any better every time I read that verse, but I clung to one thing that I truly believe God told me. He said, *"Darred, this is not the way the rest of your life will be."* And He was right. Today, I no longer walk in that depression, and I have actually found a joy that does surpass the understanding of my circumstances or the situations I have been through.

For those of you who are curious, after the four months of hell, I actually did try to pursue that young lady, and it turns out she had started dating someone else. Rather than allow myself to go back to being depressed, I got angry with God and attempted to run from Him. I attempted to chase the pursuits of the world, but this was impossible to do.

I knew the truth, the depth, and the power of His love for me; and within a couple of months, I found myself running back to Him and repenting. That young lady ended up getting married to the guy she dated after me, and truth be told, I truly wish them the best. I do not have any connection or ties with them, but if my relationship with that young lady served no other purpose than to bring me closer to God, then it was worth it. Many would look at my situation and think I was being punished for doing the right thing (because letting her go was absolutely the right thing), but I would argue that I received a reward greater than the one I was chasing after. A deeper relationship with God is incomparable to any other relationship. It may not feel like it initially, but I promise you that it is true.

After that relationship attempt, I was a bit more cautious in my pursuits of a spouse. I made a decision to not make hasty decisions to "get to know" young ladies interested in me, if I did not share that interest. Once again, I thought I was doing the right thing, but many girls became bitter of me—accusing me of not giving them a chance or opening up to the possibility of a relationship, which is not true at all.

There have been a few (literally, a few, like three) young ladies I have been interested in pursuing, and I did just that, pursued them. Yet if I felt like there was resistance or reservations within the first few weeks to a month. I was very upfront with them that I did not think it was a good idea to continue the relationship. At that point, these young ladies accused me of "leading them on" or not giving them the time of day. Once again, I thought I was doing the right thing—better to let someone go after five weeks as opposed to five months, right?

None of this seemed to matter. No matter which option I chose, I was doing it wrong. I could either accept the first girl that was interested in me, or I was a jerk for basically acting like none of these ladies were good enough for me, which is so far from the truth. It is ridiculous! I have met some incredible young ladies in the past two years, but the long and short of it is that they have simply been not right for me. I believe that the future husbands of some of these young ladies would be some of the luckiest guys on earth! They're just simply not for me.

I must say doing the right thing but feeling like it is wrong is not exclusively limited to relationships. I remember being younger and living with two other roommates, one of which was at the time unemployed. His unemployment checks had run out during the time we were living together, and he was unable to pay his part of the rent. His pursuit of looking for a new job had been lackluster at best. I had bided my time and made sure I was not angry or in a foul mood when I had approached him about the situation. We sat down, and I spoke with him about the importance of finding a job and the urgency of his situation. I was quick to quote to him 2 Thessalonians 3:10, which states, "For even when we were with you, we gave you this rule: 'The one who is unwilling to work shall not eat.'" I did the best I could to speak in an even tone and stressed that his number one priority should be to find work and not settle on anything less.

In my eyes, this was once again the right thing to do. The Bible even talks about iron sharpening iron and brothers sharpening one another. I thought this young man would be grateful that I felt our relationship was close enough to share an honest opinion with him. After giving my impassioned and very well thought out speech, his only response was, "Darred, I don't feel like you are telling me this out of love." WHAT! As Tina Turner would say, "What's love got to do with it!" He was unemployed and, if it was not for me picking up his slack on the rent, was on the verge of homelessness. And he had the audacity to say I was not being loving enough? Not loving enough would have been kicking him out the first time he could not pay rent, but I did not do that. As a matter of fact, he would live there rent-free for three months. Once again, doing the right thing did not feel like the right thing.

Situations like that would arise on many occasions. I knew that someone needed the right word or guidance, and when I shared it, I would be chastised for not extending enough grace or love. It is time for another one of Darred's bold declarations—none of us is allowed to demand grace! *Grace* is defined as "the free and unmerited favor of God, as manifested in salvation of sinners and the bestowal of blessing"—the key phrase there being "unmerited favor," which means it is not deserved or earned. It means that if we get it, it is above and beyond what we deserve. Yet at the same time, if we do not receive it, we should not be upset because we do not deserve it. When I get pulled over by the police for speeding (and I know I was speeding, mind you), it is a huge blessing when I get a warning instead of a ticket. That's grace! I deserved a speeding ticket, but I had unmerited favor with the officer when he or she decided not to give me a ticket. But let's be honest, we all still get upset when we get a speeding ticket even though we know we were speeding.

So yes, it is nice when we do something wrong, and our Christian brothers and sisters give us grace. We were wrong, and they were kind enough to overlook our transgressions. Yet I would like to clarify that I was not judging my roommate—simply pointing out an area that he needed to resolve. I did not even tell him to get his act together. I only wanted him to be encouraged, motivated, and yes, even corrected. (In my defense, he was watching entire seasons of shows in one day, and this was before binge-watching was a thing!) It was the right thing, but I was being chastised as being wrong.

This feeling is not only limited to people who are also fellow Christians. I had been told numerous times by people who did not know Jesus that following Jesus was stupid (like my roommates when I first rededicated my life). I would make decisions to give to the church or dedicate my life to ministry and would be scoffed at for not pursuing a nobler career or a more lucrative profession. Unsaved people seemed to be my biggest critics, and they also seemed to be the ones who are not afraid to share their opinions.

Now, you have to understand the flip side of this notion as well. There have been plenty of times when I have been a culprit of this crime as much as a victim. There were moments when people would share with me the direction God was calling them or things they were commanded to do to be obedient to God, and I would chastise them for foolish decisions. Yet as I have grown, I have learned that sometimes the best thing to do is to hold my tongue and simply redirect every situation back to Jesus. No matter how crazy it seems, I want to be someone who encourages someone to go to Jesus. He can definitely do a better job directing anyone than I can.

I could continue with other stories when doing the right thing seemed wrong, but I think you get my point. We live in a world that constantly tells everyone they should do whatever feels right, whatever they think is right. And I can honestly say, that's wrong! Not everything that you do with the best intentions will be received with the best response. But that's okay because Jesus even warned us about this happening. In John 15:18–19, Jesus says, "If the world hates you, keep in mind that it hated me first. If you belonged to the world, it would love you as its own. As it is, you do not belong to the world, but I have chosen you out of the world. That is why the world hates you." So you see, there are going to be times when following Jesus will make you feel like what you are doing is wrong, and that's okay!

There is not a lot I could say to put your mind at ease other than that verse, but I will take a moment to encourage you. Even in those instances when I was told that what I was doing was wrong, I remained steadfast—not all the time, but I have been getting better at it. And the great thing about it is that eventually that feeling of being wrong has always faded away. I can honestly say that in the moments I did the right thing and was told I was wrong, I have never regretted making that decision. Sure, there may have been an initial shock at the negative response, or even a twinge of anxiety that I may have made the wrong decision; but at the end of the day, I have always felt reassured by God, knowing that the right thing is always right, no matter how wrong it may feel at the time.

With that being said, the opposite is also true. Just because the wrong thing feels right, it does not make it right. That has actually been a major underlying point of this entire book. For a long time, my decisions were based on what I felt as opposed to what I believed. This is a very important concept to understand because it shapes the formation of every decision we make.

There will be cases in life where the right thing feels right and the wrong thing feels wrong, but those are easy decisions. It is when our feelings or emotions contradict what we know to be right or true that the challenge comes in. So for me, the measure of right and wrong cannot be based on my feelings. In many cases, it cannot even be based on my own conscience because I can tend to be a fairly selfish and self-centered person at times, and that's not right. So I depend on the Bible and the wisdom God gave me in the Bible to make the correct decisions, and thus far, it has not let me down. I am pretty confident that it won't let you down either.

12

———◦◦◦——

When You're Carrying the Weight of the World, Remember Who's Carrying You

This is it! The final chapter, the culmination of all the work and effort you have put in to endure my stories, bad jokes, and life lessons. And for some reason, I picked the most generic lesson regarding being a Christian and trusting God. There are coffee mugs with this "lesson" on it. Every person on earth has been told at some point, "God's got you." It is hardly the life-altering, completely unknown mystery of God's love. Yet I chose this lesson to end on. Why would I do that?

Simple—because it is the most absolute important lesson I have learned in my almost three-decade tenure on this planet! It is just as important today as it was the very first time I learned about this "God" who wanted to have a relationship with me and was willing to give up His Son to have that relationship with me. Don't worry. I will be keeping this one short because I believe that God can do a much better job of reminding you of this lesson than I ever could, but I am getting ahead of myself. Before I elaborate, please indulge me by allowing me to share with you one last personal story.

In the last chapter, I told you about the darkest season of my life, the four months when I was beyond depressed. Granted, looking back on it, the reason behind me falling into that depression is far from mind-blowing—a girl. (Cue: excessive eye-rolling here. Believe me, I feel the same way.) Part of me wishes it was a culmination of all my life's hardships hitting me all at once, and this heartbreak was simply the "straw that broke the camel's back." Or maybe I am just really bad at breakups, and this was the worst example of it—the world may never know. (I really hope it's the first one though.)

Anyhow, as I shared earlier, for four months I was chronically and inconsolably depressed, but as time went on, I gradually got better. During this time, I was also facing a myriad of other life decisions. I had just gotten accepted into my doctoral program (still working on it in fact. Woo-hoo!) and because of that, working as a full-time teacher and being a full-time student did not seem like a good idea. So I had already committed to my current job as a teacher that I would be moving on at the end of the school year. The problem was that I did not have another job lined up. I had a few different options, but nothing concrete. I was also convinced I would end up with that young lady still (still rolling my eyes from earlier), so I wanted to move to South Florida, go to the church she went to, and eventually win her back. (I know. I know! Give me a break. I was really depressed at the time!)

So that's what I did—I started my doctorate, left my job as a teacher, moved back down to South Florida where my family was, starting attending that church, and started trying to redevelop my friendship with this young lady.

Only to discover that doing a doctorate is hard. The job I had lined up didn't work out. I really was not very connected to that church, and that young lady now had a new boyfriend whom she was very happy with. Now I should preface that at this point, I had *just* gotten out of that depression and had barely recovered at this point. So a relapse seemed not only probable but would seem almost guaranteed by anyone else's standards. Yet this time, I went back to Darred's "old reliable" response, I got very, very, very angry!!!

How could I have possibly been so stupid to think that God would work everything out! How could I have been so blind to think that everything would wrap up perfectly! Why would God even care about someone as insignificant as me! Why would He give me anything I want in my life! Because if He really loved me, I would have never been depressed in the first place! Mind you, this is *after* having *all* the experiences and previous eleven life lessons I have shared in this book. But there is always a point where everyone will begin to question it all, myself included. I threw all these words at Him and was ready to make a decision to completely leave Him, to go at it on my own, because I had tried loving Him and serving Him; and I had absolutely nothing to show for it!

To be completely honest, that's exactly what I did. For about a month, I walked away from God and tried to go back to life I lived before. Life was a party, and I had missed out on about seven years of fun, and I was going to attempt to catch up on all the fun. So I decided to travel, and I drove to different states, hanging out with different people who would let me crash with them.

Now I don't want to diminish the severity of those who make a conscious decision to walk away from God, but my experience this time around was laughably bad! The "problem" (if you could call it that) was that all of my friends were Christians, so when I was driving around to different states, there was not a huge amount of opportunities to get into trouble. I think within the course of five weeks, I drank a total of five times and got drunk maybe two of those times (hardly the "bad boy" that I had been during college).

The craziest part of the whole thing was that I felt worse during this time than I had ever felt before—not depressed like I was prior to this, but just miserable. I knew that I was not having fun, and there was nothing good about what I was doing. I was just a little child, acting out against my Heavenly Father because I didn't get my way, and I knew it.

When I got back from my mini-road trip, I had another conversation with God; this time with a much different tone. I told Him I was sorry for leaving. I was sorry for doubting Him, and I asked Him to forgive me for what I had done wrong. Basically, I repented. The last part of that conversation was what I wanted to share here. Up until this point, I had blamed God for everything that had gone wrong in my life—being born to parents who didn't care for me, being abused as a child, being rejected, struggling with abandonment issues, constantly trying to be accepted based on achievements, and generally not feeling loved at times. Yet this time, after asking God to forgive me, I made a realization! And the realization was that all the pain I went through (well, most of it. I didn't choose my biological parents) was my fault!

I can still remember sitting there, telling God I had messed up my life too much for Him to fix. I told Him I was too hurt to be healed (chapter 1). I told Him that no amount of time would heal the wounds I had endured (chapter 2). I told Him that too many bad things had happened to me to be loved by Him (chapter 3). I told Him that life was too unfair for Him to waste time helping someone as bad as me (chapter 4). I told Him that my motives had always been too impure for me to be used by Him (chapter 5). I told Him I was too much of a failure for Him to create success in me (chapter 6). I told Him I was too imperfect for His perfection (chapter 7). I told Him the statistics of my life could never form a great story of His love (chapter 8). I told Him I had been called too many negative things to be called something wonderful by Him (chapter 9). I told Him I made too many mistakes to be His miracle (chapter 10). I told Him I had done too many things wrong to be made right by Him (chapter 11).

And in the moment that I felt as if everything in my world was ending and completely worthless, He showed and spoke to me. He told me, *"Darred, you can't mess up in a lifetime what I spent an eternity creating."* You see, so often Christians talk about how we are going to spend eternity in heaven with God. And that is completely true, but just as God will be in eternity after this world fades, He was also in eternity before this world was even formed. I have heard it asked so many times, "How could God possibly know everything and everyone in the world?" and the answer is so simple. "He spent an eternity preparing for it." Ephesians 1:4–5 states, "For He chose us in Him before the creation of the world to be holy and blameless in His sight. In love, He predestined us for adoption to sonship through Jesus Christ, in accordance with His pleasure and will."

We miss half of eternity when we think that eternity only happens when we pass away. Eternity happened before our lives even began. And in that time, God was able to plan and view every hardship we would go through, every trial we would face, and every hurt we would endure. And He has a contingency for every single part of it. Some of you would doubt that, even after reading this entire book; but the fact that you are reading this book, could, in and of itself, be something that God planned. Our lives are only as insignificant as we choose to make it, or they could have the greatest significance possible.

You see, my story did not start where this book began. It didn't start with the first time I was hurt. It also didn't start with the first scar I received. It didn't start with the first bad thing to happen to me. It didn't start the moment I realized life was unfair. It didn't start when I realized that motives matter more than comparisons. It didn't start the first time that I did not succeed. It didn't start when I realized I would never be perfect. It didn't start when I first recognized the statistics of my life. It didn't start the first time I recognized that God had called me. It didn't start the first time I realized I wasn't a mistake. It didn't start when I did the right thing and it didn't feel right. No, my story started the moment God decided I was worth creating.

Your story started the moment God decided to create you. The mere fact that you exist is proof enough that God wants you here. If He didn't, He wouldn't have created you. He gives you all these lessons, and He allows you to make your own decisions, for better or for worse. And the entire time, He is right there, watching out for you, caring for you, and loving you. Deuteronomy 31:6 states, "Be strong and courageous. Do not be afraid or terrified because of them, for the Lord your God goes with you; He will never leave you nor forsake you." Our lives get hard when we leave God, not when He leaves us. And when the challenges come when we are with Him—that's only because we care more about what we want than what God wants. He promised that He would never leave us, and I believe that He keeps that promise.

At the beginning of this book, I explained that it was entitled the Middle Man because everyone has felt like they have been caught in the middle of two great points in life and are stuck in a lower middle ground, where everything seems better than what we are currently going through. The fact is that all of us are middle men and women. The life we are living right now is a life between two eternities! And at times, it could feel like this life is pretty bad, but it does not have to be. The best lesson I have learned regarding being stuck in the middle is to get as close as possible to the One at the beginning and the end. (That's God, in case you haven't figured it out yet!)

So go out, live life, do things, and know that it will be messy. Know that things are not always going to go your way. Understand that it will not always be perfect. Comprehend that this is a fallen world, and that we are all messed up in some way. So when you fall short of perfection (and believe me, I guarantee that it will happen), just remember one thing—*You can't mess up in a lifetime what God spent an eternity creating.*

About the Author

D arred Williams was raised by Michael and Dawn Williams, who adopted him when he was eight years old, along with five other children who were adopted as well. He graduated from the University of Central Florida in 2010 with a bachelor's degree in political science and from Southeastern University in 2015 with a master's degree in ministerial leadership. He is currently pursuing his Doctor of Education in Organizational Leadership degree from Southeastern University. Darred has lived in Florida his entire life but has traveled all over the country, speaking to young people about how they can overcome adversity and hardship in both religious and secular settings. For more information regarding Darred or how to contact him, please visit darredwilliams.com.

CPSIA information can be obtained
at www.ICGtesting.com
Printed in the USA
FSHW021510180419
57363FS